THE STILL POINT

THE
STILL POINT

*Reflections on Zen
and Christian Mysticism*

WILLIAM JOHNSTON

PERENNIAL LIBRARY
Harper & Row, Publishers
New York, Evanston, San Francisco, London

THE STILL POINT

First PERENNIAL LIBRARY edition published 1971.

STANDARD BOOK NUMBER: 06-080227-8

To
Thomas Merton
In memoriam

Acknowledgments

Earlier versions of some of the material in this volume appeared as articles in various periodicals:

Chapter 1, "The Zen Enlightenment," appeared under the same title in *Thought*, Vol. 42, No. 165 (Summer, 1967), pp. 165–184.

Chapter 3, "Zen: Psychological Structure," and Chapter 4, "Christian Mysticism: Psychological Structure," appeared as "Zen and Christian Mysticism: A Comparison in Psychological Structure," in *International Philosophical Quarterly*, Vol. 7, No. 3 (September, 1967), pp. 441–469.

Chapter 5, "Reason and Irrationality," appeared as "Zen and Christian Mysticism: The Problem of Reason and Irrationality," in *Japan Missionary Bulletin*, Vol. 20 (1966), pp. 494–500.

Chapter 6, "Intuitive Morality," appeared as "Zen and Christian Mysticism: The Intuitive Approach to Morality," in *Japan Missionary Bulletin*, Vol. 20 (1966), pp. 608–615.

Chapter 7, "Zen and 'Amaeru,'" appeared as "Zen and 'Amaeru': Reflections on the Work of a Japanese Psychiatrist," in *Japan Missionary Bulletin*, Vol. 21 (1967), pp. 89–94.

Chapter 8, "Defining Mysticism," appeared as "Defining Mysticism: Suggestions from the Christian Encounter with Zen," in *Theological Studies*, Vol. 28, No. 1 (March, 1967), pp. 94–110.

Chapter 10, "Zen and the West," appeared under the same title in *Studies*, Vol. 56, No. 224 (Winter, 1967), pp. 349–355.

To William Collins Sons & Co., Ltd., London, and
    Harper & Row, Inc., Publishers, New York, for the
    English-language *Works* of Pierre Teilhard de Char-
    din, S.J.

To Faber & Faber, Ltd., London, and Harcourt, Brace
    Jovanovich, Inc., New York, for T. S. Eliot, *Col-
    lected Poems, 1909–1962, Four Quartets, The Cock-
    tail Party,* and *Selected Essays.*

To Princeton University Press, for the BOLLINGEN SERIES
    Collected Works of C. G. Jung.

the light is still
At the still point of the turning world
—T. S. Eliot

Four Quartets

CONTENTS

PREFACE

In the hot summer of 1968 I had the privilege of participating in the Zen–Christian dialogue held in Kyoto. This was an unforgettable experience—a week in which Buddhists and Christians met in an atmosphere of great cordiality, forming deep friendships and laying the foundations for further union. Obviously we were not in complete accord on every point. On the contrary, when it came to formulating propositions on which we agreed, it seemed that there was not a single philosophical or theological tenet that we held in common. An unbridgeable gulf appeared to separate those who believed in the soul, the Absolute, and the objectivity of truth from those who spoke of nirvana, nothingness, and the void.

Yet that we had much in common was proved by the very atmosphere of delicate charity and understanding that penetrated the week in which we lived together. And soon it became clear that what united us was not philosophy but religious experience. While in philosophical formulations we were poles apart, when it came to the discussion of values we were one. The value of deep meditation, of poverty, of humility, of the spirit of gratitude, of non-violence and the love of peace—these were things in the discussion of which we had but one heart and one soul. Indeed it was amazing that such diverse philosophies should produce such similar experiences.

Consequently the opening chapters of the book that follows deal with experience, Zen and Christian, and they attempt a psychological analysis of both, asking if a common pattern can be found. I have as far as possible dealt with the experience of modern people; for I believe that even in the great and noisy metropolis of our age there are thousands of scarcely noticed people whose psychic life is penetrated with the silent supra-conceptuality of Zen or *agape*. Only after treating of the experience have I discussed some of the theological and philosophical problems that mysticism (if I may be pardoned the use of this word) necessarily engenders. I have done this from the belief that while experience is the primary thing, we eventually must have a philosophy and a theology to protect it, circumscribe it, and distinguish the true from the counterfeit. That is why I have treated of rationality, morality, incarnation, and the rest.

The last chapters of the book say a word about the possible impact of Zen on the future of Christianity. This is a delicate point, and one that is inevitably inconclusive. Yet the fact is that not only Zen but all forms of Buddhism are going to make an enormous impact on the Christianity of the coming century. If there has been a Hellenized Christianity (which is now about to succumb with the passing of the so-called Christendom), there is every likelihood that the future will see the rise of an Oriental Christianity in which the role of Buddhism will be incalculably profound. Indeed this process has already begun. Preconciliar opposition there was; but now certain forms of Zen mediation have found their way into Japanese Christianity; they have put down roots; and no one yet knows the richness of the fruit that may well be gathered from the transplanted vine. But all is still in the experimental stage. We are still asking if a Christian *satori* is possible, how it will differ from that of Buddhism, and what the specifically Christian means to its attainment are. These are questions I have raised without adequately answering them because there is as yet no answer.

I hope that nothing I have said will lead to misunderstanding with my Buddhist brethren. I know they understand that for successful dialogue each person must maintain his own position in all frankness; and this book is written by one who believes that salvation is from the Jews—that theirs is the splendor of the divine presence, theirs the covenant, and that from them, in natural descent, sprang the Messiah. Yet this belief does not prevent me from having the highest esteem for the Buddha and for the long tradition that stems from his enlightenment. This is a tradition that has enriched the East incalculably, and I sincerely hope that it will equally enrich the West.

WILLIAM JOHNSTON, S.J.

Sophia University
Tokyo
January, 1970

THE STILL POINT

1

THE ZEN ENLIGHTENMENT

I

In recent times phenomenological study of Zen meditation has at last become possible; for now the Zen masters and their disciples have come out into the open, giving intimate records of their interior life, providing us with accurate descriptions of that inner journey which culminates in enlightenment or *satori*. It was not always so. Classical Zen is obstinately reticent; though its literature abounds in paradoxical quips and amusing anecdotes, little phenomenological detail is given about the inner process. "He that speaks does not know: he that knows does not speak" was the motto.

This reticence was to some extent broken down by Dr. D. T. Suzuki—who could scarcely be called laconic. Yet even the great old scholar, facile in prose and brilliant in paradox, gave so little phenomenological detail about *satori* and its preparatory stages that his critics tentatively expressed doubts about the depths of his experience, asking if, after all, he had attained to the highest moment of enlightenment. What Suzuki certainly did, however, was to give an enormous stimulus to Zen practice and study, with the result that numerous adventurous Westerners came to Japan in search of a *satori* that would relieve their anxiety, solve their complexes, and give a solution to the riddle of existence. Nor did these foreigners retain the old classical reserve. Magazine articles and paperbacks multiplied; and soon the West knew all about the aching legs, the face-slapping, the back-whacking, the nose-tweaking, the *"Mu . . . Mu . . . Mu"* of the *kōan*, and all the anomalous irrationalities of the topsy-turvy world of Zen. Inside Japan, too, a revival of interest in Zen took place, partly stimulated by embarrassment that foreigners should have found in Japanese culture a treasure little appreciated by the Japanese themselves.

The appeal of Zen was greatly enhanced by reports of its therapeutic effects. Zen is spoken of as a way to interior peace and harmony; it gives a certain detachment or liberation—what T. S. Eliot, in a somewhat similar context, calls "the inner freedom from the practical desire." Anyone who has spoken to a genuine Zen monk will attest to an exquisite imperturbability, a "something" that defies conceptual expression; yet something which also speaks to us through the serene Buddhas of Kyoto and Nara, through the tea ceremony, archery, flower arrangement, through every form of Japanese culture that has felt the impact of Zen; and perhaps it is this which has given rise to the saying (very true, I believe) that every Japanese is an artist. Moreover, allegedly the therapeutic effects of Zen are not only psychic. The great contemplative Hakuin is said to have recovered even his physical health through his hours and days of unrelenting meditation. Zen has been said to induce longevity and to give a certain interior exhilaration deriving from the unification of body and spirit.

Anxious to verify such reports, a group of specialists in the Department of Neuropsychiatry in Tokyo University Hospital made a detailed and scholarly study of the impact of Zen on the human body and psyche. Going to various temples, they examined Zen contemplatives (beginners and adepts, monks and layfolk) at the very time of absorption in meditation. The activity of the brain in various stages of concentration was recorded by the electroencephalograph; respiration rate was also tested, as well as the effect of Zen upon the eyesight, upon metabolism, and so on. The results of these brilliant experiments may be seen in cinematic form in Tokyo University Hospital;[1] * the general conclusion is that Zen can be very beneficial to both mind and body. Consequently it is not surprising that such an exercise should have caught the imagination of a generation longing for inner peace and release from anxiety. And so we find widespread interest in the West, and a certain revival of interest in Japan.

Among modern Japanese, Zen meditation could scarcely be called popular, sharing as it does in the general decline of things religious. "Zen is a tranquilizer," said one student to me, cynically voicing an opinion not uncommon among students that Zen and all religions are medicines or drugs to escape the difficulties of life. Yet most Japanese will evince some interest in Zen; a minority will practice it sporadically; a tiny number will go through the process, which sometimes takes decades, to its uttermost conclusion. Very few of these are seeking God in the Christian sense of that word—though, no doubt, many are seeking "something" which may in the long run approximate to the Christian "God." But why do they perform this grimly difficult exercise?

People in authority, one monk told me, feel that periods of meditation give them the moral power necessary in one who commands. Yet others, artists, feel that the spring-cleaning of the mind entailed in Zen stimulates creative activity in writing, in painting, in sculpture, or in music. Sometimes young employees are asked to begin their business career with a period of Zen to give them stamina and sticking-power in their work. Zen, again, is performed by sportsmen, as it was of old performed by the military class; for Japanese sports, such as judo, fencing, and so on, have an artistic side and demand an equilibrium which, it is said, is induced by this silent meditation. Yet others are simply looking for the moral strength to overcome the difficulties of life and to face death with courage. Zen, in-

---

[1] * Notes are listed at the end of chapters.

deed, is said to have confirmed the resolution of the
suicide pilots and of the soldiers on the field of battle
during the Second World War. Dōgen, the illustrious
founder of the Sōtō sect, declared that it was anxiety
that drove men to search for enlightenment; and today
also it is probably a deep, unsettled anxiety, leading to
a desire for liberation in truth that spurs on those who
carry Zen to its ultimate conclusion.

Obviously, then, the motives for practicing Zen will
vary a good deal according to the temperament and
disposition of the person. But one result of the increased interest has been a vast output of literature on
the Zen process. Some of this is cheap and amusing—a
pleasant diversion for the casual reader. But the vul-
garization and the rubbish written in the West should
not blind us to the great religious and psychological
value of many accounts now at hand.[2] And it is possible, I believe, with the material now available, to discover a definite pattern in the modern Zen experience,
tracing the stages through which the disciple passes in
his ascent to enlightenment. This is not to say that he
must always pass through clear-cut stages with me-
chanical inevitability—for some come to enlightenment
quickly, and others only after years of effort—but that
there is a usual path. I would like, then, to outline the
process as described by people who have gone through
it, dividing it into 1. Initial stages and the "kōan";
2. "Sanmai"; 3. "Makyō; 4. Enlightenment. It will be
clear, I believe, that Zen meditation is a process of unification in which the whole personality is harmonized
in a oneness which reaches its climax with a complete
absence of subject–object consciousness in *satori*. We
can briefly ask what this "beyond subject and object"
means.

II

It is hardly necessary here to give an exhaustive description of the initial stages of Zen meditation, already

the subject of numerous popular articles. Most people
who have dabbled a little in Zen know about the upright, cross-legged position, the gathering of the energy
in the abdomen to stimulate concentration, the deep
rhythmic breathing—all inducing a certain unity and
harmony in the personality and giving the impression
of an emptying of self. All thoughts, images, fears, feelings, anxieties, plans, ambitions, envies, whatever it
may be—all are emptied out of the mind which is reduced to the state of a *tabula rasa* like a mirror from
which every speck of dust has been removed. (When I
say "emptied," I mean that one pays no attention to
the stream of consciousness as it passes across the surface of the mind—one should not strive violently for
emptiness, for this would be futile.) Finally it is the
ego that must be forgotten in order that one may be
identified with the universe, outside space and time.
Thus there is a rejection of dualism of any kind in
search of a unity in the absence of subject–object relationship. Zen begins with a spring-cleaning of the mind.
Cobwebs are brushed away; the mirror is cleansed; the
void is created. Utter detachment from all things is demanded: Dōgen insisted that even the desire of enlightenment—the culmination of the whole process—
be annihilated; for one who is attached to *satori* has
thought and desire, and these are obstacles. Enlightenment will come, not when one ardently desires it, but
suddenly as the result of some trivial incident like the
falling of a peach blossom.

Since thinking of nothing is at first difficult, beginners may be told to count their breath—"one, two,
three," and so on—so that the mind is not dispersed but
concentrated in emptiness, while the whole personality
is calmed by the rhythmic breathing which in itself is
one of the oldest forms of therapy known. When, however, the breathing is regularized and some facility for
sitting in silent vacuity has been acquired, one may
receive the *kōan*, *Mu*. Anyone familiar with the Japanese language knows that the character pronounced *Mu*

is one of the most significant in the language, the English "nothing" being really inadequate to express what
it conjures up in the Chinese or Japanese mind. Be
that as it may, the accounts of the contemplatives
wrestling with *Mu* are an entertaining and amusing
modern adjunct to Zen literature, though they may well
cause raised eyebrows among the reserved, classical
Zennists. "Where do you see *Mu*? . . . When do you
see *Mu*? . . . How old is *Mu*? . . . What is the color
of *Mu*? . . . What is the sound of *Mu*? . . . How
much does *Mu* weigh?" are the questions asked by the
Zen Masters.[3] And the disciple goes on: "Threw myself into *Mu* for another nine hours with such utter
absorption that I completely vanished. . . . I didn't
eat breakfast, *Mu* did. I didn't eat lunch, *Mu* ate. . . .
Once or twice ideas of *satori* started to rear their heads
but *Mu* promptly chopped them off." [4] In this way
"*Mu* . . . *Mu* . . . *Mu* . . ." echoes through the Zen
experience. Not that one must make positive speculations about *Mu*—this would be fatal; rather, one must
identify oneself with *Mu* in the rejection of one's ego.

In the Rinzai sect there are other *kōan* besides *Mu*
—illogical problems kept before the mind's eye night
and day, at all times and places. Hakuin, raising one
hand, would ask his disciples: "What is the sound of
one hand clapping?" This is the famous *sekishu kōan*
which Dr. D. T. Suzuki claims led him to enlightenment. Or there is another: "Buddha preached for forty-
nine years and yet his broad tongue never moved."
And so the mockery of reason goes on. Similarly when
one goes to the master for direction, one must answer
his questions with a total neglect of, and contempt for,
logic. "A monk in all earnestness asked Jōshū, 'Has a
dog the Buddha nature or not?' Jōshū retorted, '*Mu*.' "
The answer to these questions should come not from
the mind, for reason is repudiated, but from the depth
of one's being, spontaneously like a ball bouncing back
from the wall, as one monk put it to me. There are altogether 1,700 *kōan*; but when one is solved, often

after days or weeks of grueling effort and anguish, the others may be passed through with great rapidity.

All this technique is aimed at the rejection of dualism, the repudiation of subject–object relationship. I am identified with *Mu;* I am one with the rain pattering on the roof or the cloud floating in the sky. No longer "I" and "it" or "I" and "thou," but only "is."

III

One who practices Zen meditation regularly for some time should eventually enter into a deep stage of concentration known in Japanese as *sanmai* from the Sanskrit *samadhi.* To reach this stage is a sign of progress. Normally it will begin in time of meditation, when the personality begins to be more and more unified, the eyes fixed on a point on the wall or on the ground. Ideally speaking it should continue during the day, in such wise that one is constantly seeing into the essence of things, viewing everything existentially as it is without thought of before and after, increasingly losing the sense of one's ego. Zen insists strongly on the *age quod agis* frame of mind which sees all things in their existential nudity without forethought or *arrière pensée:* that is why Zen people will often tell you that Zen is eating, Zen is walking, Zen is sleeping, and so on. But all these things must be done with a recollection that concentrates on the present moment. It is said that Dōgen, while studying in China, asked a monk: "Why don't you stay in your temple and practice Zazen instead of working in the kitchen or making such long journeys to out-of-the-way places like this just to do some shopping?" To which the monk replied: "My Japanese friend, it seems that you don't know yet the meaning of religious practice in search of the Way," and went away with a laugh. And this laconic reply, the biographer tells us, taught Dōgen that Zen is not limited to meditation but extends itself to every detail of life.[5]

The activity of the brain during *sanmai* was studied by the group of Tokyo doctors to whom I have already referred. A quotation from their report is worth noting:

> From the electrophysiological point of view, this mental state will be shown as following several points: First, during Zazen the level of the cerebral excitatory state is gradually lowered in a way that is different from sleep patterns. Second, the concentration of the mind in Zazen is superficially similar to the hypnotic trance. But there are differences in electroencephalographic findings between the two. In the mental state during Zazen, outer or inner stimuli are not neglected but precisely perceived. This is clearly shown in that there is almost no habituation in EEG responses to stimulation. These findings seem to indicate that the mental state of Zen veterans is such that it cannot be affected by either external or internal stimulus beyond the mere response to it. One master described such a state of mind as that of noticing every person he sees on the street but of not looking back with emotional lingering.[6]

The above, it seems to me, is of great interest in proving that the existential detachment the Zen masters speak of is a scientifically acceptable reality. Things are perceived indeed, for the mind is not just blank, but they are perceived without emotion, without attachment, without hate or desire—they are seen with naked existentialism, just as they are.

Obviously, too, this state is different from sleep, different from idling, different from that quietism of which Zen has sometimes been accused. In fact it is a condition of tremendous effort and concentration. One Zen adept described it to me as like the spinning of a top: so great is the activity that the top stands erect while whirling; but if the whirling slows down, it falls to the ground. And in the same way the mind, when working at white heat, stands still in silence; but when the activity slows down, it falls back to the ground of discursive reasoning.

IV

With *sanmai* one enters into the world of Zen; but the
climax is not reached without further effort and greater
suffering. As one makes progress in the silent darkness, there may arise a hallucinatory phase, when
strange phenomena rise into the consciousness. One
may see processions of Buddhist saints rising up before
one's eyes; or one may have the sensation of having no
body at all. One monk told me of the feeling that his
eye came out of his head and began to float around in
space. "As I was staying alone at home at about two
o'clock in the afternoon," writes one of Hakuun's disciples, "all of a sudden there appeared a big circle in a
corner of the room, and I saw numerous Buddhist
saints facing each other and sitting in four rows. What
a magnificent sight it was! A paradise indeed! I thought
I was surely in the land of happiness, when all at once
the figures disappeared." [7] Here is another interesting
account of one of the same disciples:

> I made up my mind to sit on until the personal in-
> terview in the morning, and concentrated my mind
> on *Mu, Mu, Mu*. I heard the clock strike three and
> shortly after that suddenly it became bright in front
> of me and I saw vividly the figure of Kannon [Avalo-
> kiteśvara or the Goddess of Mercy]. She was smiling,
> but soon she became serious and said to me: "Why
> do you delude yourself? You had better kill yourself
> if you cannot go through with this simple thing." I
> was greatly encouraged and came to myself, when the
> figure of Kannon was lost and it was completely dark
> as before. Then this was what they call "makyō," I
> thought. As I used to offer prayers to her every day,
> she must have taken pity on me and tried to save me.
> I could not but shed tears of gratitude.[8]

This period of hallucinations is known as *makyō*, which
means literally "the world of the devil." The traditional
teaching of Zen from the earliest times is that one must
simply ignore all this as being of no value or signifi-

cance. One old master has said very clearly that if you feel strange phenomena, or if you see apparitions of the Buddha or of Buddhist saints, or if you see through the wall, or find yourself able to read the minds of other people—all this is no more than the result of nervous disorder and exhaustion.[9] And his sound advice is prudently followed: the *makyō* is generally explained as the rising of unconscious elements into the conscious mind. The *kōan* or the *Mu* has checked all discursive reasoning, sweeping the mind clean of all ideas and images, with the result that mysterious, subliminal elements are now rising to the surface from the depths of unconscious life, analogously to the rising up of dreams in a deep sleep.

This stage of Zen, however, is of great significance, showing as it does how this silent meditation works at the deepest level of the human psyche, touching that unconscious life normally submerged and uninfluenced by discursive thinking. It also shows that Zen could have its dangers; for it is well known that to tamper with the unconscious can be delicate, even perilous— as is proved by the fact that not everyone is a subject for psychoanalysis. Some people's unconscious is best left unconscious. Not for nothing do the Zen people insist on the importance of a skilled director. Certainly the dangers of nervous collapse in Zen are not small, especially in the case of those who lack the strength to integrate the data rising from the unconscious or who are unable to face the basic anxiety that may be uncovered. For it seems probable that all the preparation I have described, especially the irrationality of the *kōan*, is calculated to create an artificial psychosis which may lead to the "Zen madness" that Japanese doctors know well enough, even though little has appeared about it in print in English. That enlightenment is often found by successfully passing through a psychotic experience is not just my own opinion but that of two psychiatrists of Tokyo University whom I consulted independently on this point.

However, for those who can overcome this nervous crisis the road to liberation lies open.

V

After this hallucinatory period the great climax of *satori* or *kenshō* (the word more commonly used by the Japanese, meaning "seeing into the essence of things") is not far away. It rarely comes when one is sitting silently in meditation—"Master Hui-neng, for example, got enlightenment by listening to the chanting of the Diamond Sutra, Master Teshan got it by observing that Master Lung-t'an blew a candle flame out, Master Ling-yun got it by seeing a peach flower falling, Master Po-chang got it when his master Ma-tsu twisted his nose in his young days, Master Hakuin got it by hearing the sound of the temple gong." About enlightenment little can be said that will even remotely express the reality. It is a great crash accompanied by joy and followed by deep peace. It has been poetically compared to the smashing of a layer of ice or the pulling down of a crystal tower; or the clouds have parted and the bright sun pierces through—others will say that it is as though their skull were broken into a thousand pieces. It may be worth while giving an example of the *kenshō* of a Japanese businessman, a disciple of the Zen Master Yasutani Hakuun.

Mr. Yamada describes how, going home on the train, he was turning over in his mind the words of Dōgen: "Now I have realized clearly that mind is the mountain, the river and the earth, the sun, the moon, and the stars." And, for the first time in years, he realized, with tears, that he was getting some insight into these enigmatic words. Returning to his house, he spoke with his wife and some visitors; but even while speaking the refrain kept going in his brain: "Now I have realized clearly that mind is the mountain, the river and the earth, the sun, the moon, and the stars." Later he went to bed; he continues:

I awoke suddenly in the dead of night. My mind
was not clear at first, when there occurred to me the
passage: "Now I have realized clearly that mind is
the mountain, the river and the earth, the sun, the
moon, and the stars." I repeated it; and then suddenly something like an electric shock ran through
my body, and heaven and earth collapsed. Instantaneously raptures of delight welled up in me like surging waves as I laughed aloud with my mouth wide
open, a succession of roars of laughter; "Wa-ha-ha,
ha-ha-ha, ha-ha-ha-ha-ha-ha!" "There is no need of
reasoning, no need of reasoning at all," I cried once
or twice. "Wa-ha-ha, ha-ha-ha, ha-ha-ha-ha-ha-ha!" It
was as though the sky broke open and gaped and
laughed its head off: "Wa-ha-ha-ha-ha!" My family
said afterwards that my laughter did not sound human at all.

I had been lying down at the beginning, but suddenly I sat up. My arms were striking the mattress so
vigorously that it seemed they would break, while my
knees kicked the floor so violently that it was almost
broken. "Wa-ha-ha-ha-ha-ha-ha . . . !" I threw my
head back and then lay on my face and laughed on:
"Wa-ha-ha-ha-ha-ha!"

My wife and my youngest son who were sleeping
beside me were astonished and frightened. My wife,
as I heard afterwards, covered my mouth with her
hands and cried in panic: "What's the matter with
you? What's the matter?" My son told me that he was
horrified, thinking I had gone mad. I think I heard
my wife's voice; but I don't remember at all having
had my mouth covered.

It must have been a little while after that I cried
out: "I have attained enlightenment; this is enlightenment indeed! The Buddhas and patriarchs have not
betrayed me!" How long was the interval? I feel it
was about twenty minutes; but according to my wife
it was only a few minutes. . . .[10]

The above account contains many elements typical of
the Zen enlightenment—the crash, the joy, the unification of the personality. But I would like especially to
draw attention to the quotation from Dōgen that set

the whole process in motion and brought it to its climax: "mind is the mountain, the river and the earth, the sun, the moon, and the stars." At the moment of *satori,* Mr. Yamada felt that this was really so, that there was no opposition, no duality, that his mind was identical with all things—and that reasoning was useless.

Other accounts stress that enlightenment is the result of a tremendous effort of mind and body. The eyes have been concentrated on a single point; the mind has been emptied of ideas and images; *Mu* or the *kōan* have been the center of one's life. In addition there has been lack of sleep and insufficient food; the pain in the legs has been excruciating so that perspiration breaks out over the whole body; the disciple has been beaten with the master's stick; perhaps he has been insulted, scolded, struck across the face. He may have experienced the anxiety and uncertainty of "the great doubt." Sometimes, while squatting in the lotus position, he may have been shouting at the top of his voice: "*Mu, Mu, Muuuuuuu*" as though the pent-up energy, welling up within, were exploding from the very depth of his being. And now, in a moment, everything unifies and enlightenment comes as an enormously joyful relief. The experience is followed by calm, joy, interior freedom and detachment: it gives that liberty from the shackles of worldly desire which, says Buddhism, is the source of all our suffering.

The example I have quoted may seem a little dramatic. I do not think that it is a very deep *satori* (for there are grades of depth); and it should be recalled that there are other enlightenments which are more quietly spiritual, prompted by an aesthetic experience and penetrating deeply into the personality. It should also be noted that the Sōtō sect puts more stress on gradual enlightenment, insisting that the very squatting is part of the enlightenment, not just a preparatory phase.

VI

However, the examples of *satori* I have quoted are
rather clear-cut: no one would deny that the subject
had a significant experience. But one might reasonably
ask if there are borderline cases, cases in which one may
doubt if the *satori* was the real thing demanded by
the Zen tradition. And if so, what is the norm by which
one judges if he is really enlightened? Obviously, one's
own word is not sufficient proof. No man is a good
judge in his own case—especially so, in this kind of
thing. Consequently, no matter how certain I feel about
the validity of my own *satori*, it cannot be called a true
enlightenment unless sanctioned by the word of an experienced master, himself enlightened. This sanction is
spoken of as *inka*.

All this is common-sensical enough and has a parallel
in any religion which makes a serious attempt to preserve its mysticism from deterioration. The delicate
point, however, is this: How is the master to judge?
What is his norm? This seems to have been one point
that irritated Arthur Koestler when he ridiculed the
whole thing as something quite unscientific:

> *Satori* is a wonderfully rubbery concept. There are
> small *satoris* and big *satoris*. They occur when one
> solves a *kōan*, or in meditation, but also through
> looking at a peach-blossom or watching a pebble hit
> a bamboo. The *mondōs*, in which the disciple who
> asked a too rational question is whacked on the head,
> usually end with the line: "at that moment he had
> his *satori*." Facing two famous Zen abbots in the
> Daitokuji Temple in Kyoto, I asked them how long a
> *satori* lasts. The first answered promptly: "One sec-
> ond." The second added as promptly: "It might go
> on for days." [11]

This led Koestler to the conclusion that the Zen people
themselves were not quite sure what *satori* was; he
declared that he would be justified in claiming to have

satori on each of the rare occasions when he managed to write down a sentence which said exactly what he meant; he finally dismisses the whole thing as so much "pseudo-mystical verbiage."

Certainly no clear-cut norms can be found in writing for judging the validity of *satori*. Suzuki, it is true, gives a list of the characteristics of true enlightenment, but they are so vague as to be applicable to almost any great intuitive experience. As a matter of fact, Zen on principle rejects every kind of written norm: "no dependence on words and letters" is one of its most inexorable principles; it claims to be a living tradition, something handed down from master to disciple from the very time of Bodhidharma. The key to the whole thing is the personality of the master, who can pass judgment only because he belongs to this succession of enlightened people stemming from the initial *satori*.

And he judges intuitively. He may tell at a glance, without hearing a word from the disciple. The joy and relaxation following the terrible strain may speak to him of the climax reached; or he himself may give the disciple the very blow that brings it about. All this may indeed sound sadly unscientific; but it is less disconcerting when one recalls the relationship that has existed between these two people. At the very beginning the disciple has gone humbly to a master asking for direction—a request which in olden days was often initially answered with refusals and even blows—and once accepted he has lived in the greatest intimacy with this master who has received his inner revelations, watched him closely, scolded him or struck him at the crucial moment. The disciple is even said to enter somehow into the master, so close is their relationship. They work together, eat together, sit together, the master carefully watching the inner movements of the other's soul. And after all this, it is not unreasonable to conclude that a skillful master can judge unerringly and intuitively about the validity of his disciple's experience, for he knows him through and through.

And yet one difficulty still remains—a difficulty attested to by the Zen masters themselves. And it is this: Are all the masters really competent? If the success of everything depends upon the skillful insight of the director, what happens when a director is deceived or wants to deceive others? Could there not be much chicanery in this system? What happens when a less competent master declares enlightened a disciple who, in fact, has not reached the goal? This is a subject to which Yasutani Rōshi and others constantly return; they admit that there are masters who are not real masters at all; and they confess that the modern crisis of Zen is precisely here—false judgments could lead to the creation of a series of incompetent masters which would end in the destruction of Zen.

It might be argued that what is said here of Zen is equally true of mysticism in any religion; for it is extremely difficult to find infallible norms to judge the validity of intuitive experiences. In Christianity, for example, the so-called "Rules for the Discernment of Spirits," handed down through the ages, make no claim to infallibility; and in fact Christian history abounds in examples of deluded mystics—not only neurotics and frauds but also good people, who have simply been deceived.

And yet there is one important difference here between Christianity and Zen: orthodox Christianity puts less stress on mystical experiences; and it does not build its doctrines upon them. Thus, if one were to tell, for example, St. John of the Cross that one had experienced enlightenment, the great mystic would probably answer that one should not make too much of this but should endeavor to be humble and charitable. You should believe in the Blessed Trinity, he might say, not because of what you have experienced but because of the teaching of Christ. And, moreover, in the Christian Church there would never be a question of becoming a priest or a bishop because of an experience of enlightenment. Thus, even a certain amount of mystical deceit and illusion could not unduly upset the Christian Church, whereas in Zen the whole stress is on enlightenment. If you attain to this you are a qualified teacher, you receive *inka;* you become the guide of others. For this reason it is imperative that all illusion should be controlled and excised.

VII

In order to obtain further insight into what has been said, it may be useful here to take a glance at the background from which Zen has originated.

Even to speak about "Zen background," however, has its dangers; for one is immediately entangled in the ever-recurring objection that Zen has no background, no history, no metaphysics. The Zen sect, it is conceded, may be burdened with these encumbrances; but not Zen meditation. For Zen is quite unattached; quite divorced from any system of thought; quite independent of history which it utterly transcends. When one takes up position on the *zabuton,* there should be no reasoning and talking; no questions should be asked, and if asked, they may be answered with a salutary blow; the metaphysical or historical activities of the discursive intellect, far from being a help, are the greatest obstacle to an activity which should be performed in emptiness without suppositions of any kind. This is a thesis to which Dr. Suzuki devotes many eloquent pages, invariably clinching his arguments with the clear assertion that nothing can be said about Zen except that it *is.* Dōgen, too, did not want any sectarian flavor about Zen; he objected to calling it a sect of Buddhism; for it was to be independent of all partisanship, something utterly universal: the terminology "Zen sect" was, he declared, the devil's invention.

Assuredly it might seem at first sight that, unlike Christian mystics, for whom contemplation is unthinkable without a solid grounding in Scripture and the teaching of the Church, many of the deepest Zen con-

templatives had no inkling whatever of the profundities
of Mahayana Buddhism underlying their austere practice. They simply did the job without thought and study.
Suzuki relates how the first Zen monk to whom he went
for counsel in Kamakura was totally incapable of giving
him any theoretical answer that could satisfy his mind.
Although things have changed a good deal since then
—a great number of the monks now study the Zen
classics at a university—there often remains the quiet
conviction that history, philosophy, and even Buddhism
itself have nothing to do with Zen—for this is an exercise to be practiced, not talked about. This theory is
rendered all the more plausible by the fact that in
various forms of art Japan tended to take over the ex-
ternals of Chinese Buddhism without imbibing its
spirit; so much so that the *sutras* were often chanted
in Chinese by people who did not understand their
meaning. It is easy to envisage, then, how the whole
technique of silent sitting could have been taken over
and perfected without reference to the Buddhist philosophy which gave it birth. And thus it would be
something hanging in the air, isolated from past and
future: Zen *is!*

And yet this theory has not gone undisputed. The
distinguished Chinese scholar Hu Shih reacts against
it, insisting that Zen is an integral part of the history
of Chinese Buddhism, woven into the very texture of
Chinese thought, quite incapable of being understood
outside its historical context. Certainly it is interesting
to note that Dr. Suzuki, while propounding his theory
of an "unattached Zen" outside space and time, quotes
copiously from Chinese writers whose historical value
he seems to put in question. I myself believe that traditional Zen has a background, a history, and a peculiar
spirit of its own, and that it is religious—even though
the modern tendency is to divorce it from Buddhism
and to empty it of religious content.

First of all it should be noted that the point stressed
by the majority of Zen masters is not precisely that

Zen has no background but that it is not transmitted
by words or documents of any kind. "No dependence
on words and letters" means that historical treatises and
scholarly sermons are not the means of passing it on:
it is transmitted from heart to heart. It is, in the words
of a Buddhist writer,

> the uninterrupted direct succession from master to
> disciple. In this direct succession the personalities of
> the master and the disciple are fused into one, the
> spirit being handed on from one person to the next
> without interruption. This transmission is not based
> on historical studies but on faith.[12]

And the same writer continues with a well-known
simile:

> This transmission resembles the pouring of water
> from one vessel to another in that true spirit of the
> Buddha passed on to the patriarch with neither in-
> crease nor decrease. . . . Hence it is said: "Your face
> is not your real one. The real one is transmitted from
> the Buddha." [13]

From this it is clear that there is a transmission, there
is a tradition, there is a background and a way of
thinking. The point stressed is that all this is transmitted
not by words and letters but like the pouring of water
from the vessel of the heart.

In fact anyone who has visited a Zen temple has immediately sensed a whole background of tradition and
religion. The atmosphere is permeated with it. The fre-
quent images of Shakya Muni and of Buddhist saints,
the smell of the incense, the sound of the temple gong,
the attire of the monks, the reverent silence—what is
this if not background? The great Zen contemplatives,
moreover, have possessed a certain unworldliness that
marks them out as religious men, acutely aware of the
transience of all things, filled with longing for the
eternal, living lives of devotion. And it is this whole
atmosphere that is transmitted—not by books and

words but by life. Consequently, Dr. Suzuki's unsuspecting monk, who claims that there are no suppositions in his meditation, may in fact be utterly conditioned by the surrounding Buddhist atmosphere in which he lives and by a daily monastic routine which conveys a certain spirit and roots it more deeply in the psyche than would any activity of the discursive intellect. Modern psychology teaches us clearly enough that knowledge is communicated by other means besides words and letters. The child imbibes its knowledge simply by living in close contact with its parents whose unexpressed desires, latent complexes, subconscious struggles, and suppressed ambitions are often transmitted to the deepest sectors of the child's psychic life. And it is in some analogous way, I believe, that the spirit of Zen is passed down through the monastic life of the temple and the intimate relationship between master and disciple. The whole point, then, is not that Zen has no philosophy and no history, for obviously it has, but that this history and background, reflected on discursively, does not help one iota in the attainment of enlightenment which is only found by "direct pointing at the soul"; and that the spirit is not verbalized: not written down, or systematized, or reduced to a philosophy in the Western sense. Let me illustrate this with a story taken from a chronicle of the Sung period in China:

Nine years had passed and he [Bodhidharma] now wished to return westward to India. He called his disciples and said: "The time has now come. Why does not each of you say what you have attained?"

The disciple Tao-fu replied: "As I see it, [the truth] neither adheres to words or letters nor is it separate from them. Yet it functions as the Way."

The Master said: "You have attained my skin."

Then a nun, Tsung-chih, spoke: "As I understand it, [the truth] is like the auspicious glimpse of the Buddha Land of Akshobya; it is seen once, but not a second time."

The Master replied: "You have attained my flesh."

Tao-yü said: "The four great elements are originally empty; the five *skandhas* have no existence. According to my belief, there is no *dharma* to be grasped."

To him the Master replied: "You have attained my bones."

Finally there was Hui-k'o. He bowed respectfully and stood silent.

The Master said: "You have attained my marrow." [14]

Hui-k'o had learned the true lesson. He said nothing. Yet he had imbibed the special tradition of no dependence on words and letters; the tradition of Zen was gathered up in his psychic life.

VIII

Although there are no officially written norms for *satori*, there is, however, one clear-cut characteristic which looms large in everything the Zen masters say and write—and it deserves our attention since it often brings them into conflict with Western Christians. This is the fact that enlightenment is an experience of absolute unity; it is beyond subject and object; the empirical ego is so submerged that there is no longer "I" and "it" but pure existence or "is-ness." In the preparatory stages one is constantly told that the self does not exist; that it should be annihilated; one is assured of one's identity with the universe, and at the peak one actually experiences this as true. In the example that I quoted, Mr. Yamada felt his identity with the sun and the moon and the stars. [15]

Daisetsu Suzuki goes further. He insists that this monistic submergence of the empirical ego is distinctly Oriental, whereas the "I–Thou" oppositional or dualistic (the word he prefers to use) thinking is incorrigibly Western. The Occidental (his theory states) thrives on opposition; he loves to conquer mountains and subjugate nature: the Oriental prefers to identify himself with nature and sink into it in oblivious self-effacement. In this way, Zen is the climax of a way of thinking common to Orientals—for "I" is completely gone, and only existence remains. Suzuki's way of speaking, common enough among devotees of Zen, has puzzled many Westerners who, never feeling quite comfortable unless they can classify people in tidy categories, have not hesitated to label Zen as "monistic" or "pantheistic," in spite of the protests of the masters that Zen does not fit these categories at all. What is to be thought of all this?

It may be true, as Dr. Suzuki says, that Orientals have a tendency to submerge their ego, and Westerners to stress theirs. But if it is, there are many exceptions. Apart from the Christian mystics there are intuitional schools of writers in the West who, on this point, use language which strongly recalls Zen. Let me take the example of T. S. Eliot, whose poems I had the pleasure of reading and discussing with Japanese students.

It is hardly necessary here to dwell upon Eliot's intuitive moments at the still point of the turning world —his moment in and out of time, his moment when "here" and "now" cease to matter. There has been much speculation about the nature of his aesthetic or "mystical" experiences; but in class we found a few lines which seemed to approximate to Zen. They are in *Four Quartets* where Eliot speaks of

> music heard so deeply
> That it is not heard at all, but you are the music
> While the music lasts. . . .[16]

In this typical, intense moment, music is heard so deeply that there is no longer a person listening and music listened to; there is no "I" opposed to "music"; there is simply music without subject and object, for both are submerged in one: "you are the music." Are such aesthetic experiences, when the empirical ego is so completely submerged that it no longer seems to exist, altogether uncommon? I was amazed at the facility with which my students grasped what Eliot was saying. We did not conclude that his *satori* was precisely the same as Zen but the majority did think that it was in the same psychological genus. With equal interest we read elsewhere Eliot's theory that the vocation to poetry demands a certain "depersonalization"; for the artist, aware that the mind of Europe is more important than his own personal mind, must make a continual surrender of himself to something more valuable. "The progress of an artist," he writes, "is a continual self-sacrifice, a continual extinction of personality." [17]

But let me quote another Westerner with insight into this kind of experience. Thus, C. G. Jung writes:

> To us, consciousness is inconceivable without an ego. If there is no ego there is nobody to be conscious of anything. The ego is therefore indispensable to the conscious process. The Eastern mind, however, has no difficulty in conceiving of a consciousness without an ego. Consciousness is deemed capable of transcending its ego condition; indeed, in its "higher" forms, the ego disappears altogether.[18]

We might ask, then, if the summit of Zen is one of these higher forms of consciousness in which the ego disappears altogether; and if so, it is easy to understand that people should describe it as "identity with the universe," a non-ego (*muga*) condition, and so on, using the so-called "monistic" way of speaking.

But how explain this consciousness without an ego? The Zen masters adamantly reject any attempt at explanation. Like Hui-k'o they bow respectfully and stand silent. As for Jung, he is more interested in phenomenological facts than in metaphysical explanations; but he does give a few suggestions that I shall treat of later. Then there is Eliot. He, too, nowhere treats of this problem in a strictly philosophical way; but one thing is clear: he is not denying the ontological reality of the self; he is not saying with blunt literalness

that "you are music"—he had too much common sense
for that; he is not propounding a "monism" that leaves
no room for God. No one has seriously accused the
devout author of *Ash Wednesday* of denying self and a
transcendent God. From my own reading of Eliot I
believe that his process of depersonalization is nothing
less than a way to a higher personalism; he wishes to
do away with the empirical ego in order to find a true,
universal, poetic self; he feels that our highest moments
are those in which, one with everything that is, we are
conscious of the whole universe existing in us. And that
this union with all being is compatible with distinction
from other beings I shall try to show elsewhere in this
book.

But are the Zen masters ultimately saying the same
thing as Eliot? Since they themselves refuse to speak,
it is impossible to answer this with certainty. But it is
interesting to ask the question.

Now, having examined the Zen experience, we shall,
in the following chapter, look at something parallel in
Christianity.

NOTES

1. I should like here to express my deep thanks to Professor Tomio Hirai who showed me this film and told me
   about his interesting and brilliant research.
2. In Japanese, see Yasutani Hakuun, ed. *Kyūdō no tabi,
   Gendaijin ga kataru Zen no satori no taikenden* (Travel
   in Search of the Way: Modern Men Recount the Experience of Enlightenment), First Collection (Tokyo,
   1959) and Second Collection (1962); T. Iizuka, ed.,
   Sanzen Taikenshu (Experience of the Zen Exercise),
   (Tokyo, 1956); Ishiguro Hōryū, *Zen Rigaku Yoko*
   (Summary of Zen Physics), (Tokyo, 1960). In English,
   see Heinrich Dumoulin, S.J., "Technique and Personal
   Devotion in the Zen Exercise," in J. Roggendorf, ed.,
   Studies in Japanese Culture (Tokyo, 1963); Philip Kapleau, *The Three Pillars of Zen* (Tokyo, 1965). In Ger-
   man, see Heinrich Enomiya-Lasalle, *Zen: Weg zur
   Erleuchtung* (Vienna, 1960). There are slight differ-
   ences between the Rinzai and Sōtō approaches to en-

lightenment. Yasutani Hakuun is a disciple of Harada Rōshi in whose system elements of Rinzai are incorporated into Sōtō.

3. Kapleau, *Three Pillars*, p. 227.
4. *Ibid.*, p. 228.
5. Chisan Kōhō, *Sōtō Zen* (Tokyo, 1956), p. 81.
6. In Akira Kasamatsu and Tomio Hirai, *Science of Zazen* (Tokyo, 1963).
7. Kubota Yuki, in Hakuun, *Kyūdō*, ɪɪ, p. 13.
8. Umehara Yoshitaka, *ibid.*, pp. 170–171.
9. Keizan Jōkin (d. 1325), in *Zazen Yojinki* (Warnings for Zazen).
10. Yamada Tadazo, in Hakuun, *Kyūdō*, ɪɪ, pp. 212–216.
11. Arthur Koestler, *The Lotus and the Robot* (New York, 1961), p. 243.
12. Koho, *Sōtō Zen*, p. 70.
13. *Ibid.*, p. 71.
14. Heinrich Dumoulin, S.J., *A History of Zen Buddhism*, trans. Paul Peachey (New York, 1963), p. 73.
15. See also the words of the famous Rinzai monk, Hakuin Ekaku: "It is like two mirrors mutually reflecting one another without even the shadow of an image between. Mind and object of mind are one and the same; things and oneself are not two" (in *The Zen Kōan* by Isshū Miura and Ruth Fuller Sasaki [Kyoto, 1965], p. 69).
16. T. S. Eliot, *The Dry Salvages*, lines 210 ff.
17. T. S. Eliot, *Tradition and the Individual Talent*.
18. C. G. Jung, *Psychology and Religion: West and East*, trans. R. F. C. Hull (London, 1958), p. 484.

2

THE CHRISTIAN MYSTICAL EXPERIENCE

I

There are so many varieties and shades of Christian mysticism that it would be perilous indeed to reduce them all to one system, saying: "This is the definitive Christian experience." For, as there is no established technique, there is no clear-cut path: to the end, Christian mysticism will remain something of a journey without maps. Yet spiritual writers (especially of the late nineteenth and early twentieth century which gloried in systematization) have attempted classifications which are not without value. Augustin Poulain, for example, claiming to follow Teresa of Avila, distinguishes four stages or degrees of the mystic union:

1. The incomplete mystic union, or the prayer of quiet (from the Latin *quies*, repose, which expresses the impression experienced in this state).
2. The full or semi-ecstatic union, called also by St. Teresa, the prayer of union.
3. The ecstatic union or ecstasy.
4. The transforming or deifying union, the spiritual marriage of the soul with God.[1]

And in his book, the fruit of a lifetime of experience and study, Poulain provides a vast quantity of evidence from the writings of Christian mystics to substantiate these degrees of the spiritual ascent. In this way he shows that, within certain limits, some measure of systematization is not impossible.

Much earlier than Poulain, Augustine Baker, the

sixteenth-century English mystic, distinguishes well between an "extraordinary mysticism," examples of which
he finds in Catherine of Siena and Teresa of Avila, and
an "ordinary mysticism," an example of which is *The
Cloud of Unknowing*. This latter, ordinary mysticism
can, he claims, be reduced to a system and can, to a
certain extent, be taught: it is the path trodden by a
great number of quietly unknown Christian mystics.
This, I believe, is true: *The Cloud* admirably exposes
the ordinary mystical path. But let me add that the
doctrine of its anonymous medieval author is by no
means unique: it is but one expression of that apophatic
mysticism of darkness, the fundamental principles of
which are found in Dionysius, the Rhineland mystics,
and St. John of the Cross. In modern times, a basically
similar doctrine can be found in the pages of Thomas
Merton, Jacques Maritain, and T. S. Eliot. It is mainly
this kind of mysticism that I shall speak about in the
following pages.

Before attempting any phenomenological description, however, I would like to point out that many
theologians hold that Christian mysticism is no more
than an intensification of the ordinary Christian life.
Reacting against the view that mysticism is an esoteric
phenomenon, surrounded by an aura of the occult, they
insist that it is just a deepening of that faith and love
that every true Christian possesses. They regard the
mystic as a believer who loves God so intensely that
his charity takes on a highly experimental character,
coming to possess his whole being; and if their theory
is correct, then every convinced believer is a mystic in
embryo: he already possesses a touch of Christian
samadhi and is on his way to an enlightenment which
may only reach its perfection after death.

But let us now examine how this mystical knowledge
and love usually arise in the contemplative soul.

II

The Christian life of prayer normally begins, not passively like Zen, but with active meditation on the scriptures and on the life of Christ—what the author of *The Cloud* calls "good and ghostly meditations on the passion and on one's own wretchedness." This is the so-called discursive prayer of the three powers of the soul (memory, understanding, and will) which occupies the initial stages of the life of prayer. But as progress is made, all this tends to simplify. That is to say, reasoning decreases (for a groundwork of thinking has already been laid) and one comes to rest quietly in God without laborious intellectual efforts. In this way begins what is called "affective prayer," in which one makes aspirations, acts of love of God and of gratitude, and so on—one is quietly and tranquilly with God. For one destined to go further, this simplification continues until there is only one aspiration repeated again and again in much the same way as the "Jesus prayer" of the Eastern Church. It is said that St. Francis Xavier spent whole nights repeating "My God and my All"; it is possible that Christ on the Cross reiterated "Father, forgive them, for they know not what they do." This is technically called "the prayer of simplicity"; the old authors used to regard it as the summit of what they called "ordinary prayer"; it was also called "acquired contemplation"—"acquired" because it could be attained to by one's own efforts aided by ordinary grace; "contemplation" because it was rest in one thought or idea. And this kind of prayer is generally considered the last stage prior to entrance into the mystical life.

Now, the transition to infused contemplation (which is the beginning of the mystical life) is rather simple. One has been repeating the same word or aspiration again and again (maybe thousands of times)—and then sometime one may simply pause in this rhythm and remain in silence. This is the "silentium mysticum" of the

Areopagite. It is no mere emptiness; it is ineffably rich; it is filled with the presence of Something or Someone beyond the grasp of words and ideas. The contemplative has a sense or a feeling that God is present; He is somehow here; He is in me and around me; He is dwelling in my heart; He is the very core of everything that is; and I am like a sponge in the great sea which is God. For God is somehow grasped with a sixth sense, and one knows with certainty that the world around is electrified with His divine presence and love. There is nothing to say; reasoning is useless. Indeed, for some, reasoning may be impossible, for their faculties are impeded, held by the strange presence which fills them, preventing them from acting in their usual way.

This prayer of silence is also spoken of as "dark" or "obscure," because, when the mind is void of clear and distinct ideas and images, one *knows* without being sure of *what* one knows: one does not see clearly even though the certainty of God's presence is unshakable. It is precisely this mystical darkness that is the "cloud of unknowing"; for the contemplative feels that he is in a cloud, unable to see clearly, unable to reason freely, calling out in anguish to Someone whom he cannot see but can only love. At first, moreover, this prayer is quite compatible with distractions; though one should not bother about wandering thoughts but attend to "the blind stirring of love" (the word is taken from *The Cloud of Unknowing*) quietly burning in the depths of the soul far beneath the regions of distracted discursive reasoning. This blind stirring, which John of the Cross calls "the living flame of love," is so delicately gentle that at times it is scarcely perceived by those who enjoy its presence. They simply feel a sense of helplessness, as though they can neither think nor pray; they may not realize that this situation is caused by the little flame of love, an inestimable gift of God. Sometimes, then, such people will make valiant efforts to think and reason and to make the discursive prayer they previously used; but this is useless and only makes them nervous and ill-at-ease. What they should do is to put down all reasoning beneath a cloud of forgetting (the phrase, again, is used in *The Cloud of Unknowing*), concentrating all their faculties on the living flame of love in the center of their being. The author of *The Cloud* sharply attacks those who attempt to reason and discourse when the time for silent contemplation has come. Quoting St. Richard of St. Victor, "When contemplation is born, reason dies," he protests that contemplatives who endeavor to think only kill their incipient mystical life—they are like mothers who strangle their children at birth. Let them be quiet, passive, still, expectant, calm, lest they smother the tiny flame which is their most precious possession. And so he goes on that all thoughts, all desires, all hopes, all fears, all images, all ambitions—all must be trampled down beneath the cloud of forgetting. His "forget, forget, forget . . ." reminds one of the "nothing, nothing, nothing . . ." of John of the Cross. For the latter, too, upbraids strongly those who try to think when they should remain in passive silence and love:

> There are souls who, instead of abandoning themselves to the care and protection of God, hinder Him rather by their indiscreet behaviour, or resist Him like little children who, when their mothers would carry them in their arms, struggle and cry that they may be abandoned to walk. These souls make no progress, or if they do, it is comparable only to the walking of an infant.[2]

One should not struggle against the action of God, even when it is painful and dark: "I said to my soul, be still, and let the dark come upon you / Which shall be the darkness of God."[3]

But if the contemplative remains passively attentive to this silent stirring of love, it will develop into a raging fire, possessing his whole being and governing his whole life. It will guide his actions; it will determine his decisions—self will die and the love of God will take over. The author of *The Cloud* writes:

Then that same that thou feelest shall well know
how to tell thee when thou shalt speak and when
thou shalt be still. And it shall govern thee discreetly
in all thy living without any error, and teach thee
mystically how thou shalt begin and cease in all such
doings of nature with a great and sovereign discre-
tion. For if thou mayest by grace keep it in custom
and in continual working, then if it be needful to
thee for to speak, for to eat in the common way, or
for to bide in company, or for to do any such other
thing that belongeth to the common true custom of
Christian men and of nature, it shall first stir thee
softly to speak or to do that other common thing of
nature, whatso it be; and then, if thou do it not,
it shall smite as sore as a prick on thine heart and
pain thee full sore, and let thee have no peace but
if thou do it. And in the same manner, if thou be
speaking or in any such other work that is common
to the course of nature, if it be needful and speedful
to thee to be still and to set thee to the contrary, as
is fasting to eating, being alone to company, and all
such other, the which be works of singular holiness,
it will stir thee to them.[4]

Here is a mystical love that sounds like a beautiful in-
trusion into the life of the contemplative. It is a kind
of sweet tyranny, obliging him to do God's will which
he knows intuitively; it is an almost irresistible force
against which it is useless to struggle.

III

It should be noted that this flame of love is the very
center and core of Christian mysticism. It is precisely
to foster this that reasoning and thinking are abandoned; it is to make way for this that images and desires are trampled down beneath the cloud of forgetting. Indeed, it is the vehemence of this love that im-
pedes reasoning, causing the sense of helplessness
which the mystics speak about: for all love (whether
human or divine, temporal or eternal) is intolerant of

reasoned discourse; it goes to its object with intuitive directness, abandoning roundabout paths of any kind. Hence mystical love eschews thinking: it rests in contemplative silence. And this stirring is, moreover, nothing else than a deeply experiential expression of that charity which Christ taught to be the whole essence of His message; that is why John of the Cross can speak of his doctrine as simply a commentary on the first commandment—he is teaching how to develop the mystical flame that makes one love God with one's whole heart and whole soul and whole mind and whole strength and above all things. Again, when we understand this love we get some glimmer into many of the mystical paradoxes. For love is painful and sweet at the same time so that the great Spanish mystic can exclaim: "Oh, sweet burn! Oh, delectable wound! Oh, soft hand! Oh, delicate touch!"

Love, too, explains the deep wisdom that accompanies contemplative prayer: for it would be a sad error to think of the mystical life as literally nothingness, emptiness, and negation. Empty of conceptual knowledge, the soul is filled with supraconceptual wisdom; poor in images and ideas, it is rich in a superior knowledge of God. And this mystical wisdom comes from charity. We know that in our ordinary lives, sympathy gives deep insight into the hearts of those we love; and it is the same in things divine. Love of God gives a rich wisdom. As the burning candle gives light; so does the love of God enlighten the soul—such is the traditional image. And this is what Aquinas calls the knowledge of "connaturality." In short, the silence of mystical prayer is an emptiness filled with wisdom. The void is only apparent: it is a *rich* emptiness. Emptied of reasoning, the soul is wealthy in a wisdom that comes from love.

At first the consolation of this love may predominate; but this will usually give way to pain. For one thing, the stirring of love is unifying; it is, in the words of *The Cloud*, a "one-ing exercise" in which the scattered faculties are withdrawn from their attachment to created things and fixed upon God. And this unification of the whole personality—gradually being united in itself and united with God—cannot but bring anguish. Suspended in anguish between two clouds, the contemplative cannot know God (for He is surrounded by a thick cloud of unknowing) or created things (for they are buried beneath a thick cloud of forgetting). And so, suspended in isolated anguish, the soul has only its painful love, crying out pitifully to God whom it cannot know or see: "Whither hast thou hidden thyself, And hast left me, O Beloved, to my sighing?" Indeed, the very abandoning of discursive reasoning entailed in John of the Cross's "Desire to know nothing" is itself a great sacrifice for man who naturally desiring to know (as Aristotle said so well) and to use his faculties finds great suffering in the helpless emptiness of contemplative prayer.

Yet all this suffering is small by comparison with the violent psychic reactions arising in the dark night when this love buries itself deeper and deeper in the personality. John of the Cross devotes some space to a concrete description of these "formidable trials and temptations of sense, which last for a long time, albeit longer in some than in others." The most basic and primitive passions are somehow unleashed and break out with unprecedented fury:

For to some the angel of Satan presents himself —namely, the spirit of fornication—that he may buffet their senses with abominable and violent temptations, and trouble their spirits with vile considerations and representations which are most visible to the imagination, which things are at times a greater affliction to them than death.

At other times in this night there is added to these things the spirit of blasphemy, which roams abroad, setting in the path of all the conceptions and thoughts of the soul intolerable blasphemies. These it sometimes suggests to the imagination with such violence that the soul almost utters them, which is a grave torment to it.

At other times another abominable spirit which Isaias calls "spiritus vertiginis," is allowed to molest them, not in order that they may fall, but that it may try them. This spirit darkens their senses in such a way that it fills them with numerous scruples and perplexities, so confusing that, as they judge, they can never, by any means, be satisfied concerning them, neither can they find any help for their judgment in counsel or thought. This is one of the severest goads and horrors of this night, very closely akin to that which passes in the night of the spirit.[5]

Somewhat similar descriptions can be found in the author of *The Cloud* who describes the poor soul buffeted and beaten by the stormy seas, only to be rescued by "Jesu" who walks across the waters to comfort him. Both John of the Cross and the English author urge the soul to have trust, to be calm, to remain at rest waiting for the tempest to pass. And it is in this condition that Eliot loves to tell us to sit still even among these rocks, our peace in His will. "I said to my soul, be still, and let the dark come upon you/Which shall be the darkness of God." [6]

IV

Not a few psychological explanations of this stormy night have been attempted. Modern theologians, less anxious than their forebears to attribute these upsurgings of passion to the direct action of the devil, ask the psychologist for an explication. It has been suggested that this turmoil is simply a reaction against excessive strain. For the silent prayer of contemplative love, seemingly so restful, is in fact a tremendous effort of concentration which cannot fail to make its impact on the psychic life. And it is a well-known psychological fact that a starved portion of the psyche may rebel, or that the whole organism may revolt against one-sided strain. It is hardly surprising, then, that subliminal elements should surge into consciousness with surprising violence. Or it may be that these upsurgings have much in common with the Zen *makyō*. That is to say, the silent mystical prayer has been thrusting down into the depths of the soul, extending the horizon of consciousness and integrating unconscious elements. If this is so, it fits in with an interesting description of Jung's:

> The opening up of the unconscious always means the outbreak of intense spiritual suffering; it is as when a flourishing civilization is abandoned to invading hordes of barbarians, or when fertile fields are exposed by the bursting of a dam to a raging torrent. The World War was such an invasion which showed, as nothing else could, how thin are the walls which separate a well-ordered world from lurking chaos. But it is the same with the individual and his rationally ordered world. Seeking revenge for the violence his reason has done to her, outraged Nature only awaits the moment when the partition falls so as to overwhelm the conscious life with destruction.[7]

Again, it is not impossible that these trials of John of the Cross (which have been associated with the "second conversion" in other authors) take place in many cases at a definite period in life; that is to say, in Jung's "middle period of life," a time of psychic toil and trouble occurring after the age of thirty-five. This is the age of the spiritualization of the personality, of what Jung calls a transformation of nature into culture, or instinct into spirit; and, if all goes well, it points to a coming interiority, hitherto unknown. But it is also a time of unrest, of the subconscious fear and disappointment of one who has measured out his life in teaspoons and who recoils from the specter of extinction and death that now rises before him. Hence the uncontrollable desire to create and construct before the inevitable conclusion to the drama of life. In married people this period may be accompanied by upset and wild temptations to infidelity. And at this time Jung (in words that

remind us of Eliot and John of the Cross) urges that
one be calm, quietly allowing nature to take its course
and effect the spiritualization of the personality. Among
the primitives, he claims, one so often finds "fully ma-
tured products of an undisturbed fate" whose psychic
growth has proceeded without human violence. Indeed,
Jung's "transformation of instinct into spirit" reminds
one of *The Cloud*'s passage "from bodiliness to ghost-
liness," making one ask if the turbulent night of sense
is no more than an intensified, mystical version of an
experience that other people ordinarily pass through
in their growth to maturity. And if so, this would indicate that mystical experience is not something exotic
but a deepened form of an ordinary human experience.

Be that as it may, the anguish, the trials, the upset of
the night of the senses are the factors that induce the
true mystical experience which only now begins.

V

What I have said until now, then, only refers to the
mystical life of beginners. On this point St. John of the
Cross is very clear. He depicts the trials of the night of
sense at the end of his first volume of *The Dark Night
of the Soul*, a book which is very short because the
Spanish saint is always in a hurry to get to what he
considers the real mystical experience which only begins when all these trials are over and the "house" is at
rest. There are abundant books, he tells us, describing
the initial stages (attained to by many good people),
but he wants to deal with the higher or deeper realms.
Indeed, there is a note of pathos in the warnings given
by him and other mystics about those who after coming as far as this night turn back either from fear of
the terrible suffering entailed or because they cannot
muster the courage to detach themselves from some
trifling bauble. Thus they lose the precious pearl of a
fully developed mystical life. And yet there are some
who spend the remainder of their lives in a kind of

mitigated night of sense, never fully in it and never fully out of it: the violently intense trials he has described are endured by those who are to proceed into a second night which is that of spirit.

Purified in sense, the soul is now liberated "like to one that has come forth from a rigorous imprisonment." Night being over, the same sense of the presence of God that characterized the initial stages of the mystical life descends upon the contemplative with an intensity which would be intolerable were it not filled with true peace. This is the overwhelming sense of God which unifies the faculties, sometimes causing ecstasy. It is the same flame of love that was present in the prayer of quiet; but now it has gradually descended deeper and deeper into the caverns of the soul. At first it had caused peace and joy; then it caused terrible aridity and revolt; now once again it brings a new peace. The arid desolation and storm, say the mystics, were caused by the imperfection of the soul: the log had been soaked in dampness so that it emitted smoke; it crackled as the moisture was driven out; but now, with the dampness gone, it is transformed into the flame.

The phenomenon of ecstasy is not something extraordinary, but the fruit of an intense concentration that unifies all the powers of man. So deeply and powerfully are the faculties fixed upon one object that they may become indifferent to external stimuli. To the best of my knowledge, no scientific study of the physical repercussions of contemplative prayer comparable to that made on Zen has been made; but Père Poulain, from his direction of mystical persons, was able to give the following description of ecstasy:

1. The *senses* cease to act; or they convey a confused knowledge only. According as the cessation of action on the part of the senses is complete or *almost* complete, the ecstasy is called *complete* or *incomplete*.

2. As a general rule, the limbs become immovable,

and one can neither speak nor walk nor make any gestures unless God restores this power miraculously. This last state is called *mobile ecstasy*. . . .

3. The *respiration* is almost arrested; sometimes it seems to be completely so. It is the same with the heart-beats, and consequently the pulse. In all these things there are differences of degree, according as the contemplation is more or less deep. Sometimes, at certain moments there has been ground for fearing that death has supervened.

4. The *vital heat* seems to disappear, a coldness sets in at the extremity of the limbs.

To sum up, everything seems *as if* the soul were losing in vital strength and motive power all that it gains from the side of divine union.[8]

At one time there was a certain amount of discussion as to whether ecstasy was a *necessary* stage in the Christian mystical ascent to God; but now it is generally agreed among theologians that this phenomenon is not of great significance. Its existence will depend greatly on psychological and physiological factors: some who have no ecstasy may possess a higher degree of mystical union than those who have. John of the Cross seems to be of this opinion, even considering physical repercussions of contemplation as a sign of weakness. Describing the period immediately following the stormy night of the senses, he speaks of

the raptures and trances and dislocations of the bones which always happen when the communications are not purely spiritual—that is, are not given to the spirit alone, as are those of the perfect who are purified by the second night of the spirit, and in whom these raptures and torments of the body no longer exist, since they are enjoying liberty of spirit, and their senses are now neither clouded nor transported.[9]

Traditional spiritual direction is filled with warnings against desiring such anomalies which can easily lead to illusion and self-complacence.

VI

But can we speak of a peak-point of Christian mysticism? I think not. There is no *inka*; no "this is it." No one knows how far it is possible to advance in this mystical path; no one knows to what degree the greatest contemplatives have reached. Theologians wrestled for centuries with the problem whether or not the beatific vision of the blessed was ever accorded to man in this life, some holding that Moses and St. Paul attained to this state, and others denying that it was accorded to any man. In any case this whole discussion is a priori and theological (that is, based on interpretation of Scripture and tradition) and does not give phenomenological data about a state which could be recognized as the highest point attainable by man. So while it is true that there are great moments in the Christian mystical life, it seems impossible to single out one of them, saying "This is the summit." One thing is clear enough from theology: the true goal is reached through death in eternity; any great experience attained to in life is but a shadow of a reality to come. This point is well brought out by Eliot, whose mystics, Becket and Celia, find fulfillment in heroic martyrdom. And all this points to the fact that the mystic, like any other Christian, must base his life on faith.

But there are, of course, great Christian enlightenments; and in regard to these I should like to make two points.

The first is that the experience of complete and utter unity beyond subject and object is by no means unknown in the Christian mystics. Indeed, it turns up frequently in the apophatic school about which I have said so much. The author of *The Cloud* seems to be leading his disciple precisely to something of this nature —to a state in which self is totally forgotten and there remains only God. "My will is," he writes, "that thou forget the feeling of the being of thyself as for the feeling of the being of God." And again he orders his disciple:

> Strip, spoil, and utterly unclothe thyself of all manner of feeling of thyself, that thou mayest be able to be clothed with the gracious feeling of God Himself. And this is the true condition of a perfect lover, only and utterly to spoil himself of himself for that thing that he loveth, and not admit nor suffer to be clothed but only in that thing that he loveth; and that not only for a time, but endlessly to be enwrapped in full and final forgetting of himself.

So on he goes, relentlessly insisting that the "naked knowing and a feeling of thine own being . . . must always be destroyed, ere the time be that thou mayest feel verily the perfection of this work." Here we see the loss of self and the destruction of subject–object relationship—different from Zen, however, in two ways: firstly, in that it is a union of love like that which fills the pages of *The Living Flame*; secondly, while Zen is sometimes called meditation without an object, the author of *The Cloud* speaks of meditation without a subject. Nor is this distinction merely one of semantics. To forget self so that only God remains is different from forgetting everything until only self remains.

The other point I wish to make is of some importance, though extremely difficult to express. It is that this unitive prayer, when it reaches its peak-point, contains an element of diversity or separation within the very unity. Explain it how you will, identification and separation are present at the same time. That is why the mystics like to speak of spiritual betrothal and spiritual marriage, using metaphors that bring out unity and separation, two in one flesh. It is interesting to note that certain Indian mystics, too, have spoken of the supreme experience as neither of unity nor of diversity but of something that transcends both. But the Christian mystics have almost invariably interpreted this as a reflection of the mystery of the Blessed Trinity

that speaks of identity in nature joined to separation of
persons. Yet so anguishing is this paradox that John of
the Cross and the author of *The Cloud* reserve for it
their most obscure passages which are bound to baffle
anyone who has not gone through the experience himself. The Spanish mystic seems to hold that, whereas in
the Trinity there is identification in nature and diversity
in personality, in the mystic union there is identification
in love (like the log transformed into the fire) and
separation in nature and personality. The English mystic will say that one is "naked" of self and "clothed"
with Christ (that is why, with the empirical ego gone,
one is in what Japanese call *muga* condition); but
then Christ within the mystic offers Himself to the
Father (and here is the element of separation).

Probably Eliot, too, is hinting at this in his description of his mystical heroine, Celia Copleston. Her ineffable vision is all bound up with love—a love, however, in which she finds herself in a non-self or *muga*
condition. Something or someone within her is loving
someone or something else; but both the subject and
the object of the love are indefinable. And so she ex-
claims:

> But what, or whom I loved,
> Or what in me was loving, I do not know.[10]

Here she has clearly lost her ego to such an extent that
something within her is loving something else. Small
wonder that the poor girl finds herself in a psychiatrist's
office asking what this is all about. But the psychiatrist,
astute and religious man that he is, knows that she is
perfectly sane and that her vocation is to Mount
Carmel. We know that at this period of his life Eliot
was reading John of the Cross (*Four Quartets* is full of
him), and it is difficult to escape the conclusion that
here the Son, within Celia, is loving His Father. She
has put on Christ (is "clothed" with Christ) who, in
turn, offers Himself to the Father. Hence her anguished

perplexity about who is loving whom and what has happened to her own ego.

It will be said, of course, that in all this John of the Cross, the author of *The Cloud*, and T. S. Eliot are putting a theological interpretation on an experience that allows of other, less Christian, explanations. These mystics, it will be argued, are writing theology, not phenomenology; a Buddhist might have exactly the same intuition and express it in different words in accordance with his own *Weltanschauung*. And this, I believe, is a half-truth.

On the one hand it is obviously true that the people I have quoted could not escape the influence of theology when they came to verbalize experiences which in themselves escaped all words. But on the other hand, if we accept their honesty and truthfulness we cannot reject the simple fact that the experience itself was not one of unity alone but of unity in diversity. And to support them is Martin Buber who, while cheerfully recognizing the existence of a condition of utter unity and self-forgetfulness (he even says that he himself has experienced it), confidently declares that it is not the end.

Then there is Teresa of Avila—somewhat exceptional but very interesting—in whose seventh mansion the unity-in-diversity paradox stands out boldly. On the one hand there is a loss of self couched in terms as strong as those of any Zen master. "It is as if a tiny streamlet enters the sea, from which it will find no way of separating itself, or as if in a room there were two large windows through which the light streamed in: it enters in different places but it all becomes one." [11] And yet this same Teresa, writing about the same mansion, can say that

the soul is brought into this Mansion by means of an intellectual vision, in which, by a representation of the truth in a particular way the Most Holy Trinity reveals itself, in all three Persons. First of all the spirit becomes enkindled and is illumined, as it were, by a cloud of the greatest brightness. It sees these three Persons, individually, and yet, by a wonderful kind of knowledge which is given to it, the soul realizes that most certainly and truly all these Persons are one Substance and one Power, and one Knowledge and one God alone.[12]

There is no doubt here about the unity and separation: union and separation between the Persons of the Trinity, union and separation between Teresa and her God.

It would be overly ambitious to make a metaphysical effort to unravel these paradoxes, and we may leave the matter to Teresa's "wonderful knowledge." What can be said is that the whole thing is less disconcerting when viewed against a background of Christianity's greatest mystic. What happened during those long nights of prayer on Mount Tabor can only be guessed at; but one thing is clear—the mysticism of Jesus was Trinitarian. "And suddenly the heavens opened and he saw the Spirit of God descending like a dove and coming down on him. And a voice spoke from heaven, 'this is my Son, the Beloved; my favor rests on him.'" Father, Son, and Spirit were three: and they were one. The experience of Jesus was of the most intimate union: for He was divine. Yet there was separation too: for He never said "I am the Father." What He said was: "I and the Father are one." And He declared:

Do you not believe
that I am in the Father and the Father is in me?
The words I say to you I do not speak as from myself;
it is the Father, living in me, who is doing this work.
You must believe me when I say
that I am in the Father and the Father is in me.

Here is the unity in diversity that is reflected in the lives of His mystics. The paradoxes will always remain; they will never be solved.

NOTES

1. Augustin Poulain, s.j., *The Graces of Interior Prayer: A Treatise on Mystical Theology*, trans. Leonard L. Yorke-Smith (London, 1912 [reprinted London, 1951]), p. 53.
2. St. John of the Cross, *The Ascent of Mount Carmel*, ed. E. Allison Peers (Westminster, Md., 1949), Prologue.
3. T. S. Eliot, *Four Quartets* (New York, 1943).
4. *A Tretyse of the Stodye of Wysdome* by the Anonymous Author of *The Cloud of Unknowing*; ed. Phyllis Hodgson (Early English Text Society; Oxford, 1958), p. 75.
5. John of the Cross, *The Dark Night of the Soul*, ed. E. Allison Peers (Westminster, Md., 1949), Bk. I, ch. XI.
6. Eliot, *Four Quartets*.
7. Jung, *Psychology and Religion*, Vol. 2, p. 344.
8. Poulain, *Graces*, pp. 166, 167.
9. John of the Cross, *Dark Night*, Bk. II, ch. II.
10. T. S. Eliot, *The Cocktail Party*, Act II.
11. Teresa of Avila, *The Interior Castle*, ed. E. Allison Peers (New York, 1961), "Seventh Mansion," ch. 2.
12. *Ibid.*, ch. 1.

3

ZEN: PSYCHOLOGICAL STRUCTURE

I

If Zen has made a world-wide appeal, this is partly because it seems to hold a key to the understanding of the
human mind, whose baffling mystery has caught the
imagination of our century as never before. Whereas
the medieval man looked out on an external world in
which he found magic and mystery, modern man has
found all the mystery within; and, acutely aware of his
archetypes and of the repressions simmering in the subliminal depths of an unconscious with its alternately
strangely ludicrous and bewitchingly beautiful contents, he wonders if the nuclear age has not discovered
that the most mysterious space and the most remarkable universe is within the cavernous depths of his own
mind. And the silent descent of Zen seems to throw
some light on these deep, subliminal layers. But before
asking how this is so, at the risk of being trite I would
like to recall a few ordinarily accepted facts about the
psychic life of man.

Our thinking is an extremely complex matter. We do
not just think on one layer of consciousness; for beneath
the stream of thoughts and images flitting across the
mind are other layers of consciousness, barely percep-
tible, sometimes imperceptible, but nevertheless working as truly as the contents of the conscious mind. In
short, we are not just thinking on one plane but on
many planes simultaneously: it is as if there were several rivers, superimposed one upon another, flowing in
their separate beds—though sometimes one will flow

into another causing disturbance, storm, upset, or troubled ripples. The mind may be compared to a sea with many undercurrents, some of which may rise occasionally to the surface. Or again it has been compared to a gigantic iceberg with only a fracton of its enormous bulk jutting out of the water—while the great mass, the support of everything, lies deep, deep down, many fathoms below the surface—except that the submerged part of the mind is sometimes more like a potential volcano than the quietly submerged portion of an iceberg. Modern thought sees the working of the mind less like the logical and reasoned soliloquies of Hamlet, more like the tangled and disordered jungle in the heart of Leopold Bloom.

In the unconscious mind strange things are lurking. Here are repressed memories, ugly experiences of the past, half-forgotten traumas, fears that cannot be faced, suffering that cannot be endured. What the unconscious contains in a given case no one knows; and the psychoanalyst who opens it up takes the awful responsibility of either resolving a hidden complex or raising to the surface the murkiest secret which may well bring the patient to the border of despair. Yet the unconscious may contain more than ugly things. Jung, in a passage where he is attempting to show that Zen meditation brings to the surface beautiful elements of the psychic life, reminds us that modern psychotherapy has succeeded in breaking away from the prejudice that the unconscious harbors only infantile and morally inferior contents:

> There is certainly an inferior corner in it, a lumber-room full of dirty secrets, though these are not so much unconscious as hidden and only half forgotten. But all this has about as much to do with the whole of the unconscious as a decayed tooth has with the total personality. The unconscious is the matrix of all metaphysical statements, of all mythology, of all philosophy (so far as this is not merely critical), and of

all expressions of life that are based on psychological premises.[1]

Moreover, if Jung's theories are correct, below the conscious mind and the personal unconscious is yet another layer: the collective unconscious which houses the archetypes, those quasi-Platonic, quasi-ideas of potentialities which give birth to myth and art, music and literature. I think his vision of the mind is well illustrated by one of those great Jungian dreams in which he found himself going down, down from the top storey of an old house, his own house, to the very basement where he found two old, half-disintegrated skulls; and later he saw the human mind as this large mansion in which is gathered up the past from primordial times: for not only each person's individual history but the whole history of mankind has left its imprint on the psychic life of man.[2]

Without asserting that Jung's theories are true in every detail one can agree that he gives a picture which truly reflects the complex profundity of the mind. Furthermore, he was the first great Western psychologist to interest himself in Oriental religions with all their ramifications—so we shall now look at Zen from within the framework of his philosophy.

II

In Zen the conscious mind is, to all appearances, brought to a standstill. The stream is halted; it is blocked; instead of entertaining pictures and images I endeavor to be *Mu* or "nothing." Or, alternatively, I smash the reasoning process with the illogical problem called the *kōan.* And in this way, the conscious mind is either swept clean of all pictures, remaining in total darkness, or else it is rendered incapable of thinking. Viewing this situation a priori, one might say that such a mind, totally emptied, should lapse into uncon-

sciousness; or one might suggest that voiding the mind
might induce sleep. But a posteriori we know that neither of these things happens in Zen. Rather does a new
type of mental concentration set in; and the mind begins to work vigorously at another level. I have called
this thinking "vertical," as opposed to the ordinary
"horizontal" thinking when images are flitting across the
mind.[3] Thinking vertically, the stream of images halted,
the mind goes down, down, down. . . . In other words,
the horizon of consciousness is extended, broadened,
deepened; or, put in another way, the unconscious
comes up. This explains the *makyō*, these strange appearances from the unconscious rising up as though
from another world; for we do not know what inhabits
the deep of our own mind: phantoms from the unconscious are like the witches that greeted Macbeth—they
are totally unexpected, and yet they may answer to a
scarcely realized longing or desire.

But the lower lumber room of *makyō* is still a superficial realm of the mind. Going further and further
down, one reaches a still point where peace reigns even
while above there may be storm. That is why the Zen-
influenced philosopher Nishida could write the *waka*:

> There's something bottomless
> Within me I feel.
> However disturbing are the waves
> Of joy and sorrow,
> They fail to reach it.[4]

Nishida himself attained to *satori* (enlightenment); he
had reached the bottom.

In fact Zen literature is filled with a terminology that
suggests *going down*: the masters will speak of "breaking through" (*miyaburu*) as though Zen were a mighty
effort to break through layer after layer of consciousness. And this, of course, fits in with Buddhist psychology which divides the mind into nine layers of consciousness: when one reaches the bottom layer one is
identified with the universe.

This descent of the mind into its own depths, however, is never achieved without great suffering and anxiety. In the Zen exercise an acute state of frustration, bordering on neurosis, has been deliberately fostered by the beating, the scolding, the pain in the legs, the lack of food and sleep—but, above all, by the *kōan*. For this latter illogical problem has trapped the mind in such a way that, unable to find an outlet, it is overcome with almost intolerable anguish. Well did Dōgen say that anxiety is what drives men to seek enlightenment. And it is when all the outlets are thus blocked that release and relief come in the burst of spiritual energy that gives enlightenment. It is precisely the relief after stress, the calm after the storm, that leads the master to judge that enlightenment has been attained. One sometimes hears of situations psychologically similar to this in concentration camps during the war: prisoners, after months of privation and suffering, have found their problems solved in a momentary flash of enlightenment. How account for this? I would suggest an explanation, again taken from Jung.

In a passage where he is speaking of his break with Freud, the great psychologist attacks the tendency to attribute all psychic drives to a basic sexual one; and he goes on to say that this is as though a physicist were to attribute all physical energy to, say, heat.[5] In fact, in physics we speak of energy in general which manifests itself as electricity, light, heat, etc., and in the same way there is one source of psychic energy in man which can express itself in many ways—sexual, spiritual, and so on. And if one channel is blocked, the energy, normally flowing this way, will be diverted to another channel. Put concretely (this is now mine, not Jung's), fasting may increase intellectual and spiritual activity, thus helping prayer, as also will sexual abstinence, since the energy saved will be diverted to a higher channel. Now returning to Zen: in the state of complete frustration to which he is reduced, with the outlets for instinctive energy all blocked up, the Zennist's energy

thus saved is channeled into the unconscious which
erupts into conscious life, bringing about *satori*. This,
at any rate, is a tentative solution.[6]

III

As can be inferred from what I have said, Zen fasci-
nated Jung. Not only did he write his well-known foreword to one of Suzuki's books, but he constantly
evinced great interest in the revival of Zen in Japan,
according an interview to Professor Shin'ichi Hisamatsu
shortly before his death. Put briefly, Jung's interpretation was, as I have indicated, that Zen makes the
unconscious conscious, leading to an integration of the
whole personality and abolishing conflicts that might
exist between the conscious mind and elements in its
subliminal depths. Thus he accounted for its healing
power. He felt, moreover, that Zen had a very natural
and human basis, and, though he was very chary about
the application of Zen methods to Western man, he
believed that many people in the West do attain to
satori. Let me say a little more now about his theory.

Jung's opinion that mysticism touches a new, ordinarily unactuated consciousness was not, of course, entirely
new. Already at the beginning of the century, William
James had a somewhat similar view. Our ordinary rational consciousness which occupies our waking hours,
he wrote, is only one special kind of consciousness,
while all around it, separated from it by the flimsiest
screens, there are potential forms of consciousness of a
completely different nature.[7] Just as our universe is surrounded by other universes about which we still know
virtually nothing and which may be quite different
from ours, so is the universe of the conscious mind surrounded by other potential universes. And in mystical
experience, he held, these untapped realms of the
psyche are brought into action. It should be noted,
however, that James is speaking of mysticism in general: he seems to have known little about Zen which

became popular in the West only with the arrival of Suzuki. Also interesting is his theory that the drunken consciousness is closely allied to these mystical regions, as though indicating that alcohol could bring about a state of consciousness similar to mysticism. This line of thought subsequently found interesting development in the hands of Aldous Huxley and others.

Jung's way of speaking is not so different. For him, consciousness is like an island surrounded by the sea. But he quickly points to the inadequacy of his own metaphor: for consciousness, unlike the island, is constantly being invaded by the unconscious from which, indeed, it took its origin.[8] Mystical experience, then, is something like reclaiming land from the sea, in that it is a broadening or deepening of the horizon of consciousness.

Jung makes it very clear that in *satori* what comes up is a quite new consciousness, something different from anything experienced before. In answer to the objection that enlightenment may simply be the acquisition of a new idea, as when one turns over the page of a book and sees a new picture with the same eyes, he says: "The blotting out of one picture and its replacement by another is an everyday occurrence which has none of the attributes of a transformation experience. *It is not that something different is seen, but that one sees differently.* It is as though the spatial act of seeing were changed by a new dimension." [9] In short, something new happens, affecting the whole personality and outlook.

Put more concretely, what he is saying is this: Our ordinary consciousness is greatly restricted; the amount of data it can hold is limited; when one set of ideas enters, others fall out. Tiny indeed is the field of consciousness. We possess, however, a vast amount of knowledge which is not actually present in the conscious mind—to say nothing of the treasures in the unconscious. Now, what would happen if all restriction were removed and the contents of conscious and uncon-

scious were simultaneously to enter our field of awareness? Here Jung's words are worth quoting:

> What would happen if an individual consciousness
> were able to take in at a single glance a simultaneous
> picture of every possible perception is beyond imag-
> ining. If man has already succeeded in building up
> the structure of the world from the few distinct things
> that he can perceive at one and the same time, what
> godlike spectacle would present itself to his eyes if
> he were able to perceive a great deal more all at once
> and distinctly? This question applies only to percep-
> tions that are *possible* to us. If we now add to these
> the unconscious contents—i.e., contents which are not
> yet, or no longer, capable of consciousness—and then
> try to imagine a total vision, why, this is beyond the
> most audacious fantasy. It is of course completely
> unimaginable in any conscious form, but in the un-
> conscious it is a fact, since everything subliminal
> holds within it the ever-present possibility of being
> perceived and represented in consciousness. The un-
> conscious is an irrepresentable totality of all sub-
> liminal psychic factors, a "total vision" *in potentia.*[10]

Truly this total picture is a "godlike spectacle." Jung,
in words that recall the Zen masters, say that the bottom is knocked out of a pail. Indeed, it seems impossible to express this type of experience without using
words indicating *depth.* And that is why I have called
this kind of thinking "vertical," since it opens up a
region of the mind which is ordinarily submerged.

Going on to explain the nature of the new consciousness now found, Jung says, my ego "is no longer experienced in the form of a broader or higher ego, but in
the form of a non-ego" [11] and again he declares that the
experience is *"a breakthrough,* by a consciousness limited to the ego-form, into the non-ego-like self." [12] All
this, of course, is linked with Jung's distinction between
the empirical ego and the self. The former, the empirical ego, is that "I" which we know and experience in
everyday life but which is, to some extent, illusory.

That is to say, most of us build up an image of an ego that we want to exist, an ego constructed by our vanity and desire to be something, while our real self (some notion of which is grasped by those around us who see objectively) is quite different. And this empirical ego must be destroyed if we are to find the true self.

Now Zen seems to be one way of losing the empirical ego and finding the "non-ego-like self"; for now there is no opposition between myself and the object; now I become the object (as Eliot became the music); and all relationships are replaced by the "is-ness" of pure existence. When speaking of this loss of the ego in the experience of pure consciousness, Jung refers to similar phrases of the Rhineland mystics and he quotes the famous example of St. Paul, who, in his words "I live, now not I but Christ liveth in me," seemed to have lost his own private ego in favor of the ego of Christ.

And all this points to the fact that an experience beyond subject and object is a reality which cannot be denied. There are, I believe, many types of such experiences (that of the Rhineland mystics and the Zen monks have specific differences), but they are in the same psychological genus. And this is a section of reality that comes greatly to the fore in Japanese culture wherein the notion of "becoming the object" is central. In this experience the empirical ego is lost in that state called *muga* or "non-self." Japanese also speak of two egos, the big ego (*taiga*) and the small ego (*shōga*). It is, of course, the latter that is lost. But what is one to say about the *taiga*? How explain it? This is a subject that calls for much more thought and reflection than has been given it. But perhaps it means the fullness of personality. Perhaps it means to say that I reach the peak-point of my manhood, not when I stand distinct from, and in opposition to, the universe, but when I realize my oneness with the universe. Perhaps it is the acute realization that the soul of man is, in a sense, all things (*intellectus est quodammodo omnia*). Perhaps it is the realization that my personality is not confined within the walls of this small body, this small brain, with this small coterie of friends, and so on, but becomes the universe one is living in. What greater definition of personality could we find? [13]

IV

As a therapist, however, Jung was principally attracted by the healing power of Zen; he often speaks of the psychic "wholeness" accruing from its practice. As conflict was caused by disharmony between the unconscious and conscious mind, so this was solved by the rising up of conscious elements, not only in the moment of *satori* but in the quietness of *samadhi*. For this eruption is not an indiscriminate something popping up from the mysterious depths, but is rather "the unexpected, comprehensive, completely illuminating answer" to the problems of one's psychic life. Hence the resulting equilibrium and peace.

But even (continuing with Jung) in those who have no special psychic problems Zen can promote psychic health, a deepening of the personality, a wholeness which is of great human value. This is because this making-conscious of unconscious elements is something which ought to happen if human growth goes on properly; and Zen is thus aiding and, perhaps, accelerating a process which is altogether natural. To illustrate Jung's notion of growth to emotional maturity let me quote some of his own words:

The unconscious is the matrix out of which consciousness grows; for consciousness does not enter the world as a finished product, but is the end-result of small beginnings. This development takes place in the child. . . . One can actually see the conscious mind coming into existence through the gradual unification of fragments. This process continues throughout life, but from puberty onwards it becomes slower, and fewer and fewer fragments of the unconscious are added to consciousness. The greatest and most extensive development takes place during the period between birth and the end of psychic puberty, a period that may normally extend, for a man of our climate and race, to the twenty-fifth year. In the case of a woman it usually ends when she is about nineteen or twenty. This development establishes a firm connection between the ego and the previously unconscious psychic processes, thus separating them from their source in the unconscious. In this way the conscious rises out of the unconscious like an island newly risen from the sea.[14]

Building on this theory, it is easy to see how one can come to the conclusion that Zen helps the development of healthy psychic growth, since in its silent darkness the unconscious is allowed to rise up, thus creating a deep and wealthy conscious life.

Jung, of course, is more interested in the psychological basis of Zen than in its Buddhist origins. Indeed, he seems to have regarded it as something very human with a certain degree of universality. I say this not only in view of his assertion that many people in the West get *satori* but do not speak of it because of social conditions that demand reticence, but also because a perusal of his autobiography leads me to the conclusion that Jung believed himself to have had a Western equivalent of the Zen experience. His life is taken as a gradual discovery of his real self (his Number 2, as he calls it) and he constantly refers to his visions and even to his own enlightenments. For example there is the passage in which he is giving a seminar on the *Spiritual Exercises* of St. Ignatius of Loyola and, waking up at night, he sees at the foot of his bed the figure of Christ on the Cross.

It was not quite life-size but extremely distinct; and I saw that his body was made of greenish gold. The vision was marvellously beautiful, and yet I was profoundly shaken by it. A vision as such is nothing unusual for me, for I frequently see extremely vivid hypnagogic images.[15]

One big difference between this and the *makyō* of Zen,
however, is that whereas the Zen tradition regards all
visions as nonsensical things to be rejected, Jung looked
upon his as important and significant messages from the
unconscious (though many of his critics believe he
would have been better to follow the example of the
Zen people in this) telling him of realities to come. He
claimed that a vision warned him of the coming out-
break of the First World War.

My point here, however, is that he saw interior life as
the gradual uprising of the unconscious, and explained
Zen in a similar way. His enlightenments recall *satori*.
As he writes again in his autobiography:

> What happens within oneself when one integrates
> previously unconscious contents with the conscious-
> ness is something which can scarcely be described in
> words. It can only be experienced. It is a subjective
> affair beyond discussion; we have a particular feeling
> about ourselves, about the way we are, and that is a
> fact which it is neither possible nor meaningful to
> doubt.[16]

This might seem to detract from his interpretation which
could seem to have had too much of Jung and too little
of Zen. What I believe happened was that Jung, thanks
to Suzuki, late in life stumbled upon Zen which seemed
to be a confirmation of the theories he had been propounding for many years about the human mind. Consequently he took to it with great enthusiasm but without too much knowledge of all the facts—which must,
in any case, have been inaccessible to him. But he
showed a remarkably intuitive insight into a universal
aspect of Zen and for this reason his speculations will
always be of great value.

V

Modern Japanese psychology follows the example of
Jung in exploring the therapeutic possibilities of Zen. Indeed, it is interesting and significant to note that Zen,

which penetrated almost every form of Japanese culture, should now make inroads into something so modern as psychiatry. There is the Morita therapy, for example, founded by a doctor of that name, which begins with a complete isolation of the patient from all contacts of any kind so as to create a silence and a vacuum which is the basis of cure. Dr. Morita himself, it is true, had made some unsuccessful attempts to practice Zen and disclaimed any connection between it and his system. But subsequent doctors are not so certain; and his modern successors are willing to see some connection between the two. It is hardly possible here to describe in detail the Morita system but I would like to mention the opinion of an eminent specialist on this question who sees some links between Morita therapy and Zen.

Dr. L. Takeo Doi, referring first to Morita's constant quotations from old Zen masters in support of his theories, goes on to say that Morita therapy aims at creating a state in which the mind flows smoothly and continuously without being arrested by attachment to anything; but especially it aims at the state where one is forgetful of self.[17] And this he relates to the "non-self" or *muga* of Zen Buddhism. Since the ego causes disturbance it has to be dissolved in the sense of unity with the surrounding world; Dr. Doi explains how Morita constantly urged his patients to "become the object," to become whatever they were doing. These indeed are phrases which sound strange to Western ears but are typical of the Zen mentality that has penetrated Japanese culture.

Equally interesting is the work of the distinguished Tokyo therapist, Dr. Akihisa Kondō. The principles on which he works are more or less as follows: All of us are conditioned by family background, education, upbringing, national culture, personal experiences, and so on. And all this conditioning has, so to speak, smothered the basic humanity that underlies all the dust. In the silent sitting of Zen this dust or froth is blown away in such wise that one finds one's true self, one's basic human nature, one's deepest personality. That is why the Zen people keep insisting that the object of this meditation is oneself (not a transcendent God): face to face with self one discovers one's true nature, which they call "the Buddha nature." Dr. Kondō told me that he was attracted by the *kōan* "What did your face look like before you were born?" This, he declared, is a *kōan* which brings one back beyond all conditioning to one's pure human nature. Listening to him speak I could not help recalling how the Christian mystics speak of wiping the mirror, getting off the dust so as to find one's true self in which one finds God (though, of course, the Zen masters do not go so far); or, again, of how they speak of returning to the state of original justice, discovering one's true self (call it the Buddha nature or what you will), a self more universal than the narrow empirical ego. And then the joy when one is relieved of all the baggage and conditioning accumulated in the years since birth.

I was interested to see that although Dr. Kondō stated the Buddhist principle that man lives in illusion and ignorance, he did not intend this in a literal way, as though to say that ordinary knowledge is utterly useless (Westerners so often interpret Buddhist language literally when it is phenomenological), but rather in the psychological sense or in the sense of T. S. Eliot who speaks of London as the "unreal city." That is to say: most of us live in illusion about ourselves and other people because we project upon ourselves and others the archetypes from our own unconscious. And to escape from ignorance and illusion we must discover the real self hidden below the stream of hate, fear, aggression, anger, lust, arrogance, and so on, passing across the mind. But how discover this real self? The answer is simple: Sit!

For neurotic people sitting can be almost intolerable, because in this silent vacuity problems which they normally refuse to face rise to the surface. Ordinarily they will avoid these issues, often throwing themselves into hectic work, searching for an excuse to escape their inner fears. But now there is no escape: they are brought face-to-face with what they wanted to conceal both from themselves and from others. The mental anguish may be accompanied by pains in the legs and back, strain, depression, and so on; but these are mainly psychic in origin, stemming from the agonizing confrontation with their problems. To such people Dr. Kondō recommends perseverance, sitting for ten or fifteen minutes each day, if no more is tolerable; and together with this he has personal interviews with them (for sitting alone will not effect the cure). Then gradually the irritability and anxiety of the patient may decrease; his problem, brought to the surface, may be solved in the personal interview; his will has been strengthened by the motionless sitting; the personality is unified; a certain calm sets in; the liberation of Zen is having its effect. But I would like to repeat the words with which Dr. Kondō describes how one feels:

> Actually we are not aware of mind apart from body or body apart from mind; only a total feeling of fullness exists. In this stage we are no longer separated from our sitting, so to speak.[18]

It is these last words which are so typical of Zen, and of a great section of Japanese culture. For here again we have the *muga* as I described it in the Morita system— I am no longer separated from my sitting; I become the object; I become what I am doing; I become the sitting. And in this way one finds one's true self. Dr. Kondō relates a short episode worth quoting:

> After a number of interviews I asked a patient of mine who was very much concerned that she was an illegitimate child (and who had been sitting according to my instructions), "Who were you before you were an illegitimate child?" She looked puzzled for an instant, then suddenly burst into tears, crying out, "I am I! Oh, I am I!"[19]

This seems to be the state when the dust of conditioning is wiped away and one finds one's true human nature.

To sum up, then, an examination of the psychological structure shows Zen as a system for inducing a kind of thinking which I have called "vertical" because the mind, void of concepts and images, seems to go *down* into its own silent and dark depths. If Jung's theory is correct, this entails the opening-up of a new realm of consciousness in such wise that the enlightened person does not see different things but sees differently: he is transformed.

There can, of course, be many kinds of enlightenment, such as those referred to by T. S. Eliot, Aristotle, and other great thinkers.[20] Or, again, we know that intense strain on the physical organism may sometimes bring about an explosion like that of Zen—when man, exhausted in mind and body, suddenly finds relief in a tremendous interior unification with great joy and happiness. And all these are forms of "breaking-through" to a deeper level of consciousness, the culmination of vertical thinking. The special characteristic of Zen, however, is the *muga*: the ego is lost—not lost in the type of Yoga concentration in which consciousness, drained of all content whatsoever, remains "pure" or blank without an ego; but rather lost because of the identification of subject and object. Consciousness is undifferentiated.

Though Zen as practised in the Buddhist temple has a deeply religious background, examining its psychological structure, one finds that it has a universal and deeply human aspect. That is to say, it may induce a psychic growth which *ought* to take place in human nature if all goes well in psychological development; and it brings about an enlightenment linked up with human nature as such rather than with any religious belief. In the analysis of Zen to which I have referred, Jung asserts that *satori* is altogether a natural experience; far from doing violence to human nature, it is an expression of the highest development of manhood. Perhaps something similar is meant by the Zen people themselves when they say that Zen works in a circle: at first one sees mountains as rivers and trees as mountains; and finally (after *satori*) one again sees mountains as mountains and rivers as rivers and trees as trees—only now one's picture of them is unsullied by the illusory elements which normally accompany human knowledge.

This naturally raises the question whether Zen could be divorced from Buddhism. Enomiya-Lasalle believes that it can. He believes that enlightenment has been attained to, not only by great figures like Plotinus, but by simple and unsuspecting persons who work in the fields; but that the triumph of Zen Buddhism is to have found a system for inducing something which others have only stumbled upon.[21] This is an observation of great significance in assessing the relationship between East and West as well as in the building up of Japanese Christianity. For it seems to be a psychological fact that there is a certain type of temperament which naturally inclines toward this vertical thinking and longs for it. Jung speaks of types whose consciousness is shallow but wide, and those whose consciousness is narrow but deep. The former are those who can amass a large amount of factual knowledge; the latter are the mystics. They *go down;* they acquire wisdom rather than knowledge; they relish a few things rather than take in a great number of things. And this is the type, found in the East and the West, found among Buddhists and Christians, that looks for something like Zen for personal fulfillment.

NOTES

1. Jung, *Psychology and Religion*, p. 552.
2. C. G. Jung, *Memories, Dreams, Reflections*, trans. Richard and Clara Winston (New York, 1963), p. 159.
3. William Johnston, s.j., *The Mysticism of "The Cloud of Unknowing"* (New York, 1967).
4. Translated by Dr. Suzuki.
5. Jung, *Memories*, pp. 208–209.
6. Another topic of interest in Jung's theory is its implicit rejection of anything Neoplatonic. If matter and spirit were completely opposed, it would be unthinkable that they should have a common source of energy: but if (as the Aristotelico–Thomistic tradition holds) there is

one soul animating the spiritual, sensitive, and vegeta-
tive life in man, the Jungian thesis becomes very
plausible.

7. William James, *The Varieties of Religious Experience*
   (new edition; London, 1960), Lectures XVI and XVII,
   p. 374 (the Gifford Lectures of 1901).

8. See, for example, C. G. Jung, *The Development of
   Personality,* trans. R. F. C. Hull (London, 1954), p. 52.

9. Jung, *Psychology and Religion,* p. 546. The italics are
   Jung's.

10. *Ibid.,* pp. 550–551.

11. *Ibid.,* p. 542.

12. *Ibid.,* p. 543.

13. Merton speaks of the two selves in Christian contempla-
    tion: "Contemplation is not and cannot be a function
    of this external self. There is an irreducible opposition
    between the deep transcendent self that awakens only
    in contemplation, and the superficial, external self which
    we commonly identify with the first person singular. We
    must remember that this superficial 'I' is not our real
    self. It is our 'individuality' and our 'empirical self' but
    it is not truly the hidden and mysterious person in
    whom we subsist before the eyes of God. The 'I' that
    works in the world, thinks about itself, observes its own
    reactions and talks about itself is not the true 'I' that
    has been united to God in Christ. It is at best the ves-
    ture, the mask, the disguise of that mysterious and un-
    known 'self' whom most of us never discover until we
    are dead. Our external, superficial self is not eternal,
    not spiritual. Far from it. This self is doomed to disap-
    pear as completely as smoke from a chimney. It is ut-
    terly frail and evanescent. Contemplation is precisely
    the awareness that this 'I' is really 'not I' and the awak-
    ening of the unknown 'I' that is beyond observation and
    reflection and is incapable of commenting upon itself.
    It cannot even say 'I' with the assurance and the im-
    pertinence of the other one, for its very nature is to be
    hidden, unnamed, unidentified in the society where men
    talk about themselves and about one another. In such
    a world the true 'I' remains both inarticulate and in-
    visible, because it has altogether too much to say—not
    one word of which is about itself" (*New Seeds of Con-
    templation* [New York, 1961], pp. 7–8).

14. Jung, *Development of Personality,* p. 52.

15. Jung, *Memories,* p. 210.

16. *Ibid.,* p. 287. He also writes: "There are two distinct
    ways in which consciousness arises. The one is a mo-

ment of high emotional tension, comparable to the
scene in *Parsifal* where the hero, at the very moment
of greatest temptation, suddenly realizes the meaning of
Amfortas' wound. The other is a state of contemplation,
in which ideas pass before the mind like dream-images.
Suddenly there is a flash of association between two apparently disconnected and widely separated ideas, and
this has the effect of releasing a latent tension." This
latter seems to approximate Zen.

17. L. Takeo Doi, "Morita Therapy and Psychoanalysis,"
    Psychologia, 5 (1962), pp. 117–123; also of great in-
    terest in this matter is the same author's "Psychoana-
    lytic Therapy and 'Western Man': A Japanese View,"
    International Journal of Social Psychiatry, Congress Is-
    sue (1964).
18. Akihisa Kondō, "Zen in Psychotherapy: The Virtue of
    Sitting," *Chicago Review,* 12 (1958), No. 2.
19. *Ibid.*
20. In *The Nichomachean Ethics,* Bk. X, Aristotle refers to
    moments of contemplation (*theoria*) when man's life is
    like that of God.
21. Enomiya-Lasalle, *Zen: Weg zur Erleuchtung.*

4

CHRISTIAN MYSTICISM:
PSYCHOLOGICAL STRUCTURE

I

When we come to speak of the psychological structure of Christian mysticism, another question naturally arises: does orthodox Christian theology demand that we take into account a new factor—namely, grace? Scripture and tradition make it clear that prayer is taught by God and performed under the guidance of His grace; it is not something stirred up by man with his own Pelagian efforts. So does this mean that, in a psychological study, one has to keep bargaining with the interference of a Third Party? If so, the whole question becomes extremely complicated, difficult, and delicate.

As a matter of fact, this difficulty is less formidable when we understand what modern Catholic theology teaches about the working of grace. Theology insists, of course, that not only mystical prayer but any kind of prayer at all cannot be performed without grace. St. Paul declares that no one can even call on the Lord Jesus without divine assistance, and St. John's Gospel says that the Holy Spirit dwells in the just, guiding, directing, and comforting them. This does not mean, however, that grace is interfering with the ordinary working of man's psychological categories; grace is no heavenly wrench thrown into the earthly works. Usually it will not fall under the observation of phenomenology at all. "You have not chosen me, but I have chosen you," said Christ to His disciples at the Last Supper, as though to warn them that although they *thought* they had freely

elected Him, there was at work in their psyche a hidden
force, the presence of which they did not, and perhaps
could not, suspect. Consequently, we can take it that, in
ordinary circumstances, grace is not the subject of phenomenological study: its presence is known chiefly by
faith and is studied by the theologian. To say that supernatural grace could be observed under the microscope of clinical psychology would be theologically
childish and scientifically untenable.

Besides, it would be theologically erroneous to ex-
clude the presence of grace in non-Christian mysticism.
As Rahner puts it:

> Who is to say that the voice heard in earthly phi-
> losophy, even non-Christian and pre-Christian philos-
> ophy, is the voice of nature alone (and perhaps of
> nature's guilt) and not also the groaning of the crea-
> ture who is already moved in secret by the Holy
> Spirit of grace, and longs without realizing it for the
> glory of the children of God? [1]

Consequently, in studying mystical prayer, psychology
and phenomenology can prescind from grace without,
of course, denying its presence. Indeed, the theologian
should presume that the greater part, perhaps all, can
be explained by ordinary psychological laws (which he
believes to be God's laws); for without exceedingly
good evidence no one should assert that God is tamper-
ing with the normal working of the human psyche. But
now let us examine the psychological structure of
Christian mysticism.

II

In the Christian mystics, one finds mainly two terminol-
ogies. First of all there is that of scholastic philosophy.
This speaks of "outer senses" which intuitively establish
contact with the external world, conveying sense-knowledge to the imagination which is "dematerialized" by
the so-called active intellect (*intellectus agens*)—the

faculty which accounts for the spirituality and universality of thinking—and grasped by the passive intellect (*intellectus possibilis*), now actuated by the impressed species (*species impressa*). In this way, sense-knowledge paves the way for the activity of man's highest faculties, his intellect and will. Such a system as this, highly analytical, owes much to Aristotle; it is an excellent explanation of discursive thinking and reasoning.

Many of the mystics, as for example Teresa of Avila, scarcely familiar with all the subtleties of Aristotelianism, use this terminology rather freely, sometimes substituting the Augustinian "three powers of the soul" (memory, understanding, and will) for the two highest faculties I have mentioned. To describe the prayer of quiet they will say that the *will* is lovingly fixed on God; the *memory* is occupied with His love too; the *understanding* is in darkness; the *imagination* (the fool of the house) romps and frolics wildly where it wishes. All this, as can be seen, is a very analytic description of an extremely simple experience. Something roughly equivalent is found in *The Cloud* where the author depicts the "blind stirring of love" beating constantly on the cloud of unknowing with silent fascination: the intellect is in darkness (the *cloud* means precisely this); and the wild and wanton wits, starved of their natural food of reasoning, scream out against the frustrating impediments of these two clouds of unknowing and forgetting. Or again John of the Cross speaks of the purification of the *will* which is to possess only the love of God, purification of the *intellect* which is to be filled only with the darkness of God in faith, and purification of the *memory* which is to be filled only with hope in God.

Yet in some ways this terminology is not entirely satisfactory. For one thing, it is too analytical to describe mysticism which is an experience of unity. Again, it is geared to a reasoning process which it explains admirably. But in the deepest prayer there is no reasoning, but only an ineffable stirring in the deepest center of one's being that can scarcely be called either knowledge or love, for it is a delicate blend of both. And, moreover, this terminology does not make allowance for *depth* in the mind; and Christian mystical experience, like Zen and psychoanalysis, cannot escape from the sense of profundity or "going down." In the prayer of quiet, for example, there seems to be an inescapable consciousness of two levels of the mind working at the same time. Up above, the imagination is working wildly, running amuck, while below at a deeper point one is silently and lovingly concentrated on God. The author of *The Cloud* describes this by speaking of how the devil rattles the outer windows violently, while inside the poor little soul sits quietly in the house, quite unperturbed. Or again, using an age-old metaphor, he compares this silent prayer to a sleep in which "the wild ghostly wits" are bound and utterly voided "so that the silly soul may softly sleep and rest in the lovely beholding of God as He is." [2]

Even in less advanced forms of prayer this consciousness of two levels of the mind is so common as scarcely to need comment. Anyone with a little experience of direction has found people who complain that they "cannot pray," that they "cannot concentrate," that their mind is filled with distractions; but in answer to the questions "Yet beneath all these distractions do you have the feeling that anything is going on? Beneath all this is there some sense of union with God?" they will often answer hesitatingly "Yes." For in their mind two processes are at work simultaneously; but the upper one is often so noisy and obstreperous as to distract from the deeper, delicate manna, the living flame of love, burning so quietly at the core of the being that its very presence may go unheeded.

It is because of this psychological situation that so many mystics turn to another way of speaking and use a different terminology in which the notion of depth is more clearly marked. The soul will be the "interior castle," the outer, noisy courtrooms of which must be passed through if one is to enter the inner mansion where the King dwells. Or one goes down into the center of one's being (into the cavernous depths of Tauler), and these deep reaches are often said to be "delicious" or "full of repose"; for this is the part of the psyche where one "tastes" and "savors" the love of God. In short, Christian mysticism, like Zen, uses a terminology of "going down" (though not with the violent "breaking through") to the ground of one's being through various layers of consciousness. Sometimes the picture of the soul is not unlike the Jungian building, with the mystic going down to the basement. T. S. Eliot expresses it well when he writes:

> Descend lower, descend only
> Into the world of perpetual solitude,
> World not world, but that which is not world.[3]

Eliot himself tells us that these words occurred to him as he was descending in the elevator in the London Underground on his way to Faber and Faber. A modern metaphor indeed!

And one could also quote yet another Christian mystic, who seems the most extrovert of them all, yet finds his true self in a silent descent. Here are the words of Teilhard de Chardin:

And so, for the first time in my life perhaps (although I am supposed to meditate every day!) I took the lamp, and leaving the zone of everyday occupations and relationships where everything seems clear, I went down into my inmost self, to the deep abyss whence I feel dimly that my power of action emanates. But as I moved further and further from the conventional certainties by which social life is superficially illuminated, I became aware that I was losing contact with myself. At each step of the descent a new person was disclosed within me of whose name I was no longer sure, and who no longer obeyed me. And when I had to stop my exploration because the path faded from beneath my steps, I found a bottomless abyss at my feet, and out of it

came—arising I know not whence—the current
which I dare to call *my* life.[4]

This "going down" process, here described by Teilhard,
turns up constantly in the mystics who speak of "the
ground of the soul," the "apex mentis," the "scintilla
animae," the "principalis affectio," the "substance of the
soul," the "center of the soul," the "Seelenfunklein," the
"core of one's being," the "sovereign point of the spirit,"
and so on. The exact meaning of this terminology (for it
differs with different authors) is not at all easy to unravel, though most of it is greatly indebted to Neoplatonism. Poulain, remarking that the mystics consider these
words sufficiently obvious to require no definition, goes
on to say that in general they regard the soul as a
sphere: on its surface are the sensible faculties but
within there is a part removed from the exterior world
and the knowledge found herein has nothing to do with
the senses, the sensible faculties, or reason.[5]

All this indicates clearly enough that Christian mysticism, like Zen, is a species of "vertical thinking" in
which, void of concepts and image, the mind spirals
down to the core of one's being. And then two problems
naturally suggest themselves. First, what causes this
"going down" process? Second, what does one find or
touch when one reaches the center of the sphere?

III

As for the first point, we have already seen that the
"descent" in Zen is caused by the emptying of the mind,
the preoccupation with *Mu,* the doubt and anxiety
caused by the *kōan,* and the general stress of the exercises. And in Christian mysticism a somewhat similar
situation has been created. For, after a long time devoted to reasoning and discursive prayer, when the early
stages of the mystical life are beginning, the mystic experiences a kind of ligature, an inability to think, as
though the energy which normally is active in the conscious mind were transferred to some deeper level of the

psychic life. At this deeper level, a unification of the personality is taking place: one is no longer "scattered" (to use the terminology of the author of *The Cloud*) but is gathered together in silent "oneness"—hence the great difficulty of discursive thought which, of its very nature, breaks up unity and occupies itself with a variety of objects. Now it is quite possible that such a unification of the personality could be effected by various kinds of concentration (as on a philosophical or mathematical problem) causing an identical psychological state; but the characteristic of Christian mysticism is that the faculties are withdrawn from the various objects on which they were "scattered" in order to be fixed on God. In short, the faculties are drawn together and unified by the love of God.

Traditional spiritual direction has never permitted the Christian to drop discursive prayer until his love for God is so strong that he finds difficulty in thinking—by reason of a constant longing for God. For difficulty in thinking and reasoning is not caused now by an emptying of the mind or by any special technique, but by the vehemence of that "living flame of love" which is the very center of Christian mystical prayer. If, as everyone knows, any kind of love is inimical to the slowness of discursive thinking, and if (even in human affairs) love flies straight to its object unencumbered by roundabout discourse, is it not understandable that the love of God will be intolerant of thinking and reasoning and cause a certain ligature?

John of the Cross tells us that in this state the memory is filled with a longing for God; and this is put more picturesquely by the author of *The Cloud* when, addressing himself to his disciple, he says that the stirring of love

> . . . goeth with thee to bed, it riseth with thee at morrow, it followeth thee forth all the day in all that thou dost, it reaveth thee quotidien from thy wonted exercise and goeth between thee and it, it commoneth and followeth with thy desire, insomuch that thou

thinkest it all one desire or thou knowest never what,
it changeth thy gesture and maketh thy countenance
seemly; while it lasteth all things please thee and
nothing may grieve thee; a thousand mile wouldst
thou run to converse mouthly with one that thou
knowest verily felt it; and yet, when thou comest
there, canst thou nothing say, speak whoso speak
will, for thou wouldst speak but of it; few be thy
words, but full of fruit and fire; a short word of thy
mouth containeth a worldful of wisdom, yet seemeth
it but folly to them that dwell in their own wits; thy
silence is soft, thy speech full speedful, thy prayer
is privy, thy pride full pure, thy manners be meek,
thy mirth full mind, thy list is liking to play with a
child; thou lovest to be alone and sit by thyself; men
would hinder thee; thou wouldst not read books nor
hear books but only of it. . . .[6]

Such is the stirring of love that hinders thinking, binds
the faculties, and promotes the descent to the center of
the soul.

But just as the final stage of the Zen breakthrough is
not achieved without doubt, anguish and the great
death, so the stirring of love will not normally do its
most thorough work without the torment of the night of
the senses with all its accompanying anguish. In addition to this, a great number of Christian mystics have
performed incredibly severe austerities which effected
their most profound mystical experiences. It is true, of
course, that later many of them regretted their excesses,
calling them imprudent and warning others not to imitate them; but it is questionable if without such austerities their mystical life would have reached fruition. Or
again one finds that frequently the deepest enlightenment has been preceded by some great crisis, some
acute humiliation, some protracted illness—something
which has shocked the personality at its deepest roots,
sending the soul spiraling down to its inmost center
where it has met God.

And this raises the second question I proposed: do the

Christian mystics meet God? Or what do they find in the deepest core of the mansion of the soul?

Here it must be confessed that the Christian mystics are as baffled as the Zennists: they cannot express what they experience; it just does not fit into conceptual language. Most of them (as we have seen) use Trinitarian language, or they will speak of divine "touches" or "wounds," or they will use other symbolic expressions. God sends out "a beam of ghostly light" which pierces the cloud of unknowing and shows to the contemplative some secrets "the which man may not and cannot speak" and which fills his affection with love; but, goes on the English author, "of that work that pertaineth only to God dare I not take upon me to speak with my blabbering fleshly tongue: and, shortly to say, although I durst I would not." [7]

And yet, beneath the mystical protest that words cannot convey the reality, there are discernible two characteristics that I would like to mention as being of significance in relation to Zen.

The first is that the notion of seeing into one's nature is by no means absent in the Christian mystics. It is by cleansing the mirror that one finds one's true self; and this true self is the image of God, for it is made in the likeness of the Blessed Trinity:

And know well that he that desireth to see God, him it behoveth to cleanse his soul, the which is a mirror in the which all thing is clearly seen when it is clean. And when the mirror is foul, then mayest thou see nothing clearly therein. And right so it is of thy soul. When it is foul, neither thou knowest thyself, nor God . . . and therefore cleanse thy mirror. . . .[8]

In this way the mystical descent is made into the deepest realms of the soul where God is—or, more daringly and correctly, which is God. For John of the Cross says that the center of the soul is God.[9]

The second point is that in many mystics the empirical ego is lost in an experience beyond subject and object. John of the Cross emphasizes that this experience is attained through love and that one's own ego is replaced by that of Christ:

> . . . it is true to say that the Beloved lives in the lover and the lover in the Beloved; and such manner of likeness does make in the transformation of the two that are in love that it may be said that each is the other and that both are one. The reason for this is that in the union and transformation of love the one gives possession of itself to the other and exchanges itself for the other. Thus each lives in the other, and the one is the other, and both are one through the transformation of love. It is this that Saint Paul meant when he said: "Vivo autem, iam non ego, vivit vero in me Christus." Which signifies: "I live, yet not I, but Christ liveth in me." For in saying "I live, yet not I," he meant that, although he lived, his life was not his own, because he was transformed in Christ and his life was divine rather than human.[10]

Here is a detailed description of that "identification" with Christ which we have already seen in the anonymous author of *The Cloud* who maintains that it is the part of a true lover to divest himself of everything he has for the loved one, and to be naked that he may be clothed with the garment which is Christ: emptied of self he is to be filled with Christ. It should be noted, however, that these authors I have quoted are not only mystics, but also theologians, and in their expressions they are attempting to express not only their moments of the highest mysticism but also the knowledge they have from faith and reason. Put more concretely, they are eschewing any form of pantheism, any indication that the "ego" may be an utterly illusory thing. Hence the obscurity which can arise in John of the Cross, who chooses his words with the greatest care:

So that, according to the likeness of transformation, we can say that his life and the life of Christ are one life through union of love, which in heaven will be perfectly accomplished in the Divine life in all those who shall merit being in God; for, being transformed in God, they will live the life of God, and not their own life, and yet it will be their own life, for the life of God will be their own life.[11]

And again:

For even as in the consummation of marriage according to the flesh the two become one flesh, as says the Divine Scripture, even as, when this Spiritual Marriage between God and the soul is consummated, there are *two natures in one spirit and love of God.*[12]

So the two natures remain distinct; the nature of man does not become the nature of God; the union is enacted by love.

Yet to understand the language of the Spanish mystic (who is here speaking as a theologian) everything must be taken in a Trinitarian context and in relation to the Incarnation. Attempting to resolve the tremendous paradox of how one can become the other while remaining oneself, he finds the solution in a Trinitarian context. For the Three Persons share the Divine Nature while remaining themselves. But this aspect has already been discussed. Suffice it to point to the descent into the center of oneself and the loss of the empirical ego.

IV

I said in a previous chapter that the uprising of the unconscious in Zen is responsible for certain visions or voices or strange experiences called *makyō;* so that the question now arises as to whether there is anything similar in Christian mysticism. And, of course, such phenomena are by no means unknown. When the mind is swept clean of thoughts and images and reduced to a blank, people of a certain temperament may find themselves confronted with visions rising up from the subliminal depths. Traditional Christian spiritual direction, keenly aware of the possibility of deception and illusion, adamantly advocated the rejection of anything of a grotesque nature. Yet the whole question of visions and extraordinary phenomena is difficult and delicate.

For one thing, there seems to be the possibility that for some people a great intuition may take the form of a picture. The idea that has come to their mind may be enacted before them very vividly. T. S. Eliot indicates such a situation when he makes his somewhat mystical Sir Henry Harcourt-Reilly (who has a keen intuition of the coming death of Celia Coplestone) say that when he first met her he saw "the image, standing behind her chair / of a Celia Coplestone whose face showed the astonishment / Of the first five minutes after a violent death"; and then he explains this pictorial phenomenon to the incredulous listener:

> If this strains your credulity, Mrs. Chamberlayne,
> I ask you only to entertain the suggestion
> That a sudden intuition, in certain minds,
> May tend to express itself at once in a picture.
> That happens to me, sometimes.[13]

Here Harcourt-Reilly's vision was no mere illusion; it was true; it was an intuition which turned out to be tragically accurate. Perhaps he was one of those people, like some great painters, who possesses such a pictorial imagination that they see in the form of a picture what others would intuit in a less vivid way. And his experience is all the more credible when one recalls Jung's assertion that something interior may seem to be exterior, and that something exterior can appear to be interior.[14]

Again orthodox theology claims that a vision may be a communication from God. To deny outright the possibility of such a divine intervention would be to contradict a long Christian tradition. Yet here again the problem is full of pitfalls; and Jung's statement which I have quoted is of great relevance. Karl Rahner, insisting that the visionary seldom sees the object in its physical reality, points with approval to the statement of Teresa of Avila that the physical body of Christ has never been seen upon the earth since the Ascension, and goes on to say that most visions are either imaginative or intellectual.[15] In short, the whole drama takes place within the mind of the visionary. But in this case what causes the vision?

Rahner answers with John of the Cross that a deeply spiritual communication of God, produced in the very depths of the spirit, may so overflow into the imagination and senses as to form a picture. And then, of course, the all-important thing is not the picture, but the spiritual communication which has given it birth. Indeed, the picture itself is not too trustworthy; it may be colored by subjective elements—an Italian mystic may see an Italian Madonna, and a German, a German *Fräulein*. This is because it is no more than a secondary repercussion, stemming from the real action of God which is working in the deepest part of the soul beyond imagery of any kind, a pictureless activity of the imageless Godhead who communicates Himself in pure spirit.

Grasping this, one can understand the wariness, even suspicion, that John of the Cross evinces for visions of any kind. He feels that they are a snare and a trap; and his "nothing, nothing, nothing" includes utter detachment from visions of any kind which, he maintains, should be abandoned in order to meet God in pure faith. Eliot, again, catches his thought well on this point when he makes his prayer for Celia at the outset of her mystical journey:

> Protect her from the Voices
> Protect her from the Visions
> Protect her in tumult
> Protect her in the silence.[16]

Visions and voices are dangers in the pure, mystical path to God.

John of the Cross, in fact, makes very clear the distinction between the communication of God and its interpretation by the mystic. The former, of course, is good, true, precious: but the interpretation may be false, since it is an attempt to put into words and images something which transcends human language. Moreover, he insists, one should not even attempt to interpret the communications of God; and if a pictorial interpretation presents itself to the senses, it ought to be rejected. This is because God's communications do their work instantaneously without the need of formulation or reflection or interpretation on our part. It is not even necessary to decide whether they are, or are not, real communications from God. One must simply proceed on one's way in complete detachment and in the darkness of faith. Attachment to any such experiences might lead the mystic to think that he had come into direct contact with God Himself. And this would be a tragic error, a demeaning of God who is above anything that man can hear or see or touch. God can only be met in pure faith, which is like night to the soul.[17]

V

If it is true that Christian mysticism has some similarities with Zen, one must necessarily ask: what about its therapeutic value? One of the principal appeals of Zen is its beneficial effect on mind and body—the euphoria, the longevity, the unification of the personality; and one may ask if Christian mysticism makes similar claims. Does the Christian breaking through layers of consciousness induce that psychic wholeness that so delighted Jung? Does it entail an integration of unconscious elements into the conscious life with a corresponding healing effect?

Until fairly recently Christians paid little attention to this point. Whereas Buddhism is rooted in a longing to escape from anxiety, from suffering and from stress in order to attain what modern psychology might call "psychic wholeness," the Christian traditionally has gone to prayer to honor his heavenly Father and to ask for daily bread. If, in this process, salutary psychic side-effects came about, so much the better. But they were secondary.

For the body, Christian mysticism has not, to the best of my knowledge, made serious claims of beneficial improvement. On the contrary, there is considerable evidence of early spiritual heroes' insisting that weak health was a necessary condition for great progress in prayer. Nor was there emphasis on breathing—the factor which, in Zen, is probably crucial in strengthening the physique. But there is often mention of psychic benefits. The author of *The Cloud* constantly comes back to the tranquil countenance and the measured gait of the true contemplative. Even the ugliest man, he says, if he find his way in contemplation, will become acceptable to all and will be loved by all. Such is the suavity that accrues from contemplation. And he seems to regard this beautiful external deportment as a norm by which one can judge the genuineness of the contemplative gift.[18]

This belief that true prayer promotes psychic health came to the fore some decades ago when psychoanalysis first broke in upon the public eye. Standing up against the seemingly new-fangled psychology, not a few spiritual writers insinuated that all neurosis (which, they claimed, was just a symptom of the disharmony between man and his Creator) could be cured by faith, by prayer, and by the sacraments. In short, the real therapy was prayer in faith.

Against this, however, arose the indignant protests of those who held that prayer could no more heal a neurosis than it could cure a broken leg: both were real sicknesses. Besides, they continued, investigation into the lives of the saints proves that neurosis afflicts not only the sinner but also the saint; for as the latter can

contract cancer and tuberculosis so he can, like other
mortals, contract deeply neurotic tendencies. It became
customary to quote Teresa of Avila and her little name-
sake of Lisieux as examples of saints who were psy-
chically sick.

It is probably true that contemplative prayer alone
cannot heal a neurosis. Nor can Zen. In the example I
have quoted, Dr. Kondō uses the silent squatting as a
help towards cure; he does not say that it alone does
the work. And some specialists of Tokyo University Hospital who have studied this question thoroughly end
their report in this way:

> Lastly, we would like to mention the relationship
> of Zazen and mental health. It is often said that
> Zazen is good for mental health. But we believe that
> Zazen alone cannot take the place of medical psycho-
> therapy, though it certainly can be used as a useful
> adjunct or supplement. Or perhaps the enlightenment
> of Zen may provide the final goal of psychotherapy,
> for one has to attain, after all, one's true "self." [19]

In this way Zen is a help. And probably the same is true
of Christian mysticism in which the same level of the
psyche is at work and in which the unconscious is purified in a very similar way. This is further substantiated
by the fact that the personality of the true mystic reveals
a certain depth and balance—which is what the author
of *The Cloud* is trying to say. Nor, of course, is this
incompatible with one of the neurotic emotional dis-
turbances (especially one originating in childhood)
which afflict such a great proportion of the human race
today. It is even possible that a deep neurotic anxiety
may be the very motivation that impels the mystic to
break through the troubled surface of his soul in search
of God, the source of peace and enlightenment.

VI

Perhaps it is now possible to recall some of the parallels
and some of the differences between Zen and the ordi-

nary Christian mysticism typified by *The Cloud of Unknowing*.

First of all the parallels. Both are forms of vertical meditation—somewhat similar processes. The silence, the rejection of words and thoughts, the obscurity or darkness of the mind, the thinking of nothing, the emptiness or the void—all point to a similar psychological state of mind in these two forms of concentration. Then there is the "going down" or descent, the breaking through various levels of consciousness to the center of the soul, the seeing into one's own nature, the loss of the empirical ego, the enlightenment experience beyond subject and object provoked by a period of intense anxiety—whether it be the dark night of the senses or the great doubt and death. Again, there is in both an attitude of suspicion toward voices and visions and psychic anomalies. Both promote some kind of psychic wholeness and unification. And people of a similar temperament seem to be attracted by both. All this indicates that as *forms of concentration* there is great similarity: the same sector of the psychic life seems to be at work.

On the other hand there is a great gulf separating them—namely, that which induces the state of concentration is in each case widely different. In Zen, as has been pointed out, this psychic state is induced by the sitting, the breathing, the irrational *kōan*, the beating, and so on—in other words, this state of concentration has been artificially provoked. And there has been a tremendous effort to get rid of all suppositions, whether metaphysical or dogmatic; whereas in Christian mysticism the suppositions have been the key to the whole thing. These suppositions are faith in, and love for, Christ which have normally been nurtured for years until (almost unexpectedly) something happens: one *cannot* think because of the vehemence of "the living flame of love" that has arisen in the heart. In short, the concentration has been induced by love rising out of faith; and traditional spiritual direction has never favored the cessation of thinking until it is convinced that the ligature has been caused precisely by love and faith and not by anything else.

The enlightenments, too, can scarcely be called the same. First of all, because one cannot divorce any great intuition from the philosophy of life that gave it birth— and in these two cases the philosophy is quite different. Secondly, insofar as they speak about it, the Christian mystics speak of a union in love (as can be seen from the passages of St. John of the Cross I have quoted) which is quite absent in Zen. And thirdly, because the Christian mystic speaks of a unity and diversity found simultaneously.

My opinion is that in Christian mysticism, in Zen, in the aesthetic experiences of a T. S. Eliot, we are touching a realm of the psychic life which has many divisions and compartments and sections: I mean that the whole field of supraconceptuality is extremely varied. To conclude that, because in a great variety of experiences the same kind of concentration and a similar loss of the empirical ego is attained to, all are therefore just the same, is an unwarranted oversimplification which satisfies neither the Christian mystic nor the Zen Buddhist. Both of these assert that their experiences are not the same.[20]

But they will agree that there is common ground for dialogue. And this is of great significance.

NOTES

1. Karl Rahner, s.j., *Nature and Grace* (New York, 1964), p. 141. Speaking of moments of grace, Rahner asserts that a person "cannot clearly distinguish them by simple reflection (by the light of natural reason) from the natural spirituality of his nature. But when once he knows through revelation that this order of grace exists, which is given to him unmerited and does not belong to his nature itself, then he will be more careful; he must take into account that perhaps many things which he concretely experiences in himself and ascribes almost involuntarily to his 'nature' are in fact due to

the working in him of what he knows from theology to be unmerited grace" (p. 136).

2. *The Epistle of Privy Counsel*, Ch. VI.
3. Eliot, *Four Quartets*, "Burnt Norton," Stanza III.
4. Pierre Teilhard de Chardin, *Le Milieu Divin* (London, 1960), p. 54.
5. Poulain, *Graces*, Ch. IX, p. 27.
6. *The Epistle of Privy Counsel*, Ch. XI.
7. *The Cloud of Unknowing*, Ch. XXVI.
8. *A Tretyse of the Stodye of Wysdome*, p. 43.
9. "The center of the soul is God; and, when the soul has attained to Him according to the whole capacity of its being, and according to the force of its operation, it will have reached the last and the deep center of the soul . . ." (*Living Flame of Love*, Stanza I, Exposition).
10. John of the Cross, *Spiritual Canticle*, Stanza XI, 6.
11. *Ibid.*, Stanza XI, 7.
12. *Ibid.*
13. Eliot, *The Cocktail Party*, Act III.
14. Jung, *Memories*, p. 268.
15. Karl Rahner, s.j., *Visions and Prophecies* (New York, 1963), p. 32.
16. Eliot, *The Cocktail Party*, Act II.
17. See, for example, John of the Cross, *The Ascent of Mount Carmel*, BK. II, ch. XVIII ff.; Bk. III, ch. CVIII, etc.
18. See *The Epistle of Privy Counsel*, Ch. XI.
19. Kasamatsu and Hirai, *Science of Zazen*.
20. Hakuun states that there are elements of Zen outside Buddhism but that they are different from the Zen he is propounding. He refers to these elements as *gedō zen*. See Kapleau, *Three Pillars*, p. 43.

5

REASON AND IRRATIONALITY

I

> The people who make the great meditations state
> questions which neither Saint Thomas nor Scotus
> could satisfactorily answer to the unbelievers.[1]

Such was the astonished comment of one of the early
Christian missionaries confronted with the seeming irrationality of Zen. To men brought up on syllogistic
scholasticism the Zen way of speaking must indeed
have seemed outrageous; and though modern philosophy is less shocked by this existentialist mockery of the
conceptual world, it is still the disconcerting paradox,
the adamantine refusal to reason, and the apparently
ridiculous, unmeaning statements that arouse the opposition and ire of the exasperated critics of Zen.

I have already given examples of the *mondō* and the
kōan; but let me add a few to illustrate the point:

> A monk asked Master Jōshū: "What is the meaning
> of Bodhidharma's coming from the West?"
> "The cypress tree in the garden," Jōshū replied.[2]

Or again:

> A monk asked Master Jōshū: "What is Jōshū?"
> "East gate, west gate, south gate, north gate,"
> Jōshū replied.[3]

Or again:

> "Empty-handed, yet holding a hoe;
> Walking, yet riding a water buffalo."[4]

Or again:

> We often hear it said: "In our sect there are no
> written letters to be set down, no words and phrases
> to be made known, no delusion to be freed from, no
> enlightenment to be attained." [5]

Here we have a few examples of a way of speaking that
characterizes the whole approach of Zen.

Yet the language of the Christian mystics can be disconcerting, too; and perhaps this accounts, in some
measure at least, for the distrust they have often en-
gendered. It is especially true that those of the apophatic way of thinking (who take their cue from Dionysius with his ray of darkness) can jolt one no less than
the exponents of Zen. The Rhinelanders, the author of
The Cloud of Unknowing, and St. John of the Cross all
have this tendency; in our own time T. S. Eliot when
he turns to paradox reaches the peak-point of his well-
known obscurity. Take, for example, this passage from
Four Quartets:

In order to arrive at what you do not know
    You must go by a way which is the way of ignorance.
In order to possess what you do not possess
    You must go by the way of dispossession.
In order to arrive at what you are not
    You must go through the way in which you are not.
And what you do not know is the only thing you know
And what you own is what you do not own
And where you are is where you are not. [6]

Words like these sound as though taken from a book
by Dr. Suzuki; but in fact they are only a faithful following of that school, the greatest exponent of which
is John of the Cross, for whom all is nothing, knowledge
is ignorance, light is darkness, and life is death.

In short, a great number of mystics, East and West,
speak a language which seems different from our own,
talk words which sound like rigmarole to the uninitiated, and give the impression of utterly disregarding

logic. The problem is how to decipher this language, how to get to the root meaning of it all.

The difficulty is rendered all the more acute by the obstinate refusal of the mystics to explain themselves. By now we are all well attuned to the if-you-don't-have-the-experience-yourself-you-don't-understand way of speaking which frustrates so many well-intentioned people. Or the attitude which says: "Do it yourself and you'll understand; words are useless; books are useless; this is something empirical, something that can only be understood when you do it." This kind of thing (found in Zen and Christian mysticism alike) has had the effect of irritating the unenlightened who feel themselves condemned to the dull and drab Platonic cave, looking always at illusory shadows while the mystics enjoy the sunshine of enlightened truth. Yet the mystics persistently say that words are virtually useless when it comes to describing an experience which is essentially beyond words. And so the thing ends in stalemate. But to many it is all suspicious. "Taken at face value and considered in itself," writes Arthur Koestler, "Zen is at best an existential hoax; at worst, a web of solemn absurdities." [7] And here he voices the opinion of a large number of people for whom Zen is only an excuse for wasting time and talking nonsense.

The exact degree to which paradox is linked to mystical experience is not easy to assess. Many Christian mystics do not use paradox at all (Bernard of Clairvaux, Ignatius of Loyola, the two Teresas, and many others could be cited), and those who do so, generally pertain to a way of thinking that owes much to Neoplatonism. In Zen, too, one could ask to what extent the paradox is central. Certainly the *kōan*, where the most disconcerting irrationality appears, is of rather late origin: there was deep enlightenment before ever it came on the scene. And Dōgen himself vigorously advocated "Zazen alone" (*shikan taza*) without appeal to the *kōan* as a means to the summit. It was Hakuin Ekaku (d. 1769) who really systematized the 1,700 *kōan;* and it is the Rinzai school which makes the greatest use of them.

However, even though one admits that paradox is not an essential element of the language of mysticism, everyone must agree that the language is mysterious and calls for explanation.

II

Confronted with this problem, one could take various positions. One theory which turns up frequently in modern psychology runs more or less as follows: since mysticism is a retreat to a new level of conscious life and the actuation of a cognitive power ordinarily latent and unused, it leads to a new realm of reality in which logic, syllogism, causality, and the rest are no longer valid. Reason, this theory holds, has no more than relative value: the highest knowledge is utterly irrational. Hence the meaningless nonsense talked by the mystics is in fact the supreme wisdom. It is quite true, then, that the ordinary, common-sensical rational man is in the murky Platonic cave: the mystics are enjoying true wisdom in the sunlight.

It should be noted, however, that this is just a modern, introspective version of a theory that goes back to the dawn of history and is deeply embedded in Oriental (especially Hindu) thought; namely, that there are two sections of reality, one of which is illusory, and the other real. When one, through enlightenment, reaches the freedom of true reality, one realizes that syllogisms, reasoning, and sense-knowledge are all false and illusory. The dimension reached by mystical experience is the only true reality.

Yet there is another possible explanation, and one that ought to give satisfaction to the enlightened and unenlightened alike. This is to hold for the reality of both worlds; to show that sense-knowledge and mystical knowledge are both valid. But to do this, one must resolve the paradoxes and explain the language of the

mystics, showing that all their extraordinary statements
are, after all, consonant with the ordinary logical laws
of human thinking. This is not easy; but it seems to me
to be the only way that could be acceptable to modern
man, who will not easily jettison reason and sense-
knowledge (which are the source not only of science
and learning but also of basic common sense), and who
at the same time has some sympathy for the mystical
approach to life.

III

In trying to solve this problem, however, it should be
kept in mind that to *transcend* reason and to *contradict*
reason are very different things. That mystical knowledge transcends reason, that it is incalculably superior
to the knowledge accruing from the discursive intellect,
every mystic will unhesitatingly assert. John of the
Cross, the author of *The Cloud of Unknowing*, and all
the rest reiterate with emphasis that *when the time has
come for contemplation* reasoning and thinking should
be abandoned in favor of a superior, supraconceptual,
and existential silence. They will keep saying that thinking is an obstacle to what they are teaching, that the
person who insists on using his faculties actively when
called to passive prayer loses something infinitely precious; they attack the spiritual director who, not understanding this kind of thing, makes his disciple stay too
long in discursive prayer. And sometimes their language
is so violent that they seem to deny the value of reason
outright; but a close examination of their words shows
that this is not their intention at all. They merely wish
to stress the beauty of mystical knowledge *by comparison with which* ordinary knowledge looks like ignorance. Dionysius (who gave the first impulse to much
of this) as well as John of the Cross were philosophers
and theologians. The notion of denying the validity of
reason never entered their heads.

And in Zen there seems to be something similar. For

here, too, the disciple is being led to a superior wisdom
of a supraconceptual nature; here, too, a tremendous
effort is made to arrest discursive thinking in order that
the psychic life may work at a deeper and more powerful level; here, too, reasoning is checked with *Mu* and
the *kōan*, and so on. Consequently, when the monk asks
"What is Jōshū?" and gets the answer "East gate, west
gate, south gate, north gate"—this may just be a way
of saying: "Don't think; don't use your discursive intellect; don't reason; true knowledge develops in a different realm of your psyche from all this." And if so, the
attitude is basically the same as that of John of the
Cross.

However, the *kōan* is not only this; it is more. It
seems to be a technique not only to check thinking but
also to create the doubt and anguish necessary for enlightenment; and in this point, there is nothing equivalent to it in Christian mysticism. The importance of
"doubt" is greatly stressed by Hakuin. "In Zen," he
writes, "he who does not bring doubt to bear upon the
kōan is a dissolute knavish good-for-nothing. Therefore
it is said: 'Underlying great doubt there is great *satori*;
where there is thorough questioning there will be thor-
oughgoing experience of awakening.'" [8] Deliberately
and artificially to engender doubt, then, is one function
of the *kōan* which is a technique to bring about a certain experience, and by no means is it meant as an ontological statement: it need not be taken as a denial of
reason.

We can conclude, then, that in many cases the language of Zen and Christian mystics is simply aimed at
inducing the would-be mystic to sacrifice discursive
meditation in favor of an intuitive knowledge which
transcends, but does not necessarily contradict, ordinary
reasoning. But, of course, there are other times when
their paradoxes are meant to have real ontological
value; and we must ask now about them.

IV

The very nature of mystical knowledge precludes expression in affirmation, denial, and concepts. This is because it is beyond concepts (the mind being emptied of all images and thoughts), and beyond the subject–object dualism demanded by statements of affirmation and denial. It is an experience of unity—of oneness with all that is in Zen, or my oneness with God in the Christian mystics. Mystical prayer is existential in the sense that (to follow the wording of the author of *The Cloud of Unknowing*) I no longer think of *what* God is but of *that* God is—and no more.[9] The peak-point of mystical experience is reached, according to this medieval English writer, when, forgetful of all clear-cut essences (and even of my own being), I am conscious of only God. And in Zen the peak-point is reached when my empirical ego is forgotten and I am conscious only of being. In short, mysticism sees the unity of all things; and how can unity be expressed in dualistic language?

Moreover, this experience is a very true one. That all things are, in fact, one was grasped from the dawn of Greek thought by philosophers who kept asking what the principle of unity in all things was, until Parmenides came up with the answer that all things are one by reason of their being. And it is interesting to see how the same idea is expressed by a Zennist in a much more poetical way. She had enlightenment and describes how, filled with joy, she went outside only to find that everything and everyone looked like a Buddha:

> People came along this way and that. They were all Buddhas, every one of them. A fair Buddha; a dark Buddha; rendezvousing Buddhas; a small Buddha; cats and dogs that looked like Buddhas; even a tiny ant caused love within me.
> Late in the afternoon I went out shopping. The street was full of Buddhas with baskets. . . .[10]

If for "Buddhas" you substitute "being" here, you find an experience not unlike that of a number of mature mystics in the West who grasped intuitively the unity of all things *sub specie entis*. All things are one; and all things are being. Or, all things are one; all things possess the Buddha nature.

Grasping the unity of all things, however, one may be tempted to deny diversity, coming thus to the position I have already mentioned that logic, reasoning, and duality are all illusory. And then, as a corollary, one could rollick in irrationalities, laughing at the poor deluded unfortunates who think that there is diversity in the universe, and inviting them (once again) to come out of the dirty Platonic cave into the sun. But other philosophers have preferred to reconcile the one and the many; and in the Aristotelian school of philosophy we find that things are one by reason of their existence and different by reason of their essence: they are one in *that* they are, diverse in *what* they are. Mystical knowledge is of one order, being existential; discursive reasoning is of another, being essential. Both are necessary.

Grasping the complementary nature of these two kinds of knowledge, one can unravel the paradoxes of the apophatic, Dionysian mystics: for their paradoxes are indeed paradoxes, not contradictions. For example, it is frequently stated that God is known by ignorance or "unknowing" and that the highest wisdom is ignorance. This way of speaking (influenced by St. Paul's 1 Corinthians but later used by mystics in a somewhat non-Pauline sense) simply means that in order to attain to mystical knowledge one must sacrifice (that is, *be ignorant of*) ordinary, discursive knowledge. One must empty the mind, putting thoughts and images beneath a cloud of forgetting; and the more ignorant one is of essential thinking the more wise one can be in existential thinking. And so is solved the paradox that wisdom is found in ignorance.

Furthermore, this wisdom is "dark" because the

mind, emptied of distinct thoughts and ideas, is in obscurity which is like darkness or night. However, this dark, existential knowledge is of immense value, since it brings one close to God who is Light and "so the darkness shall be light, and the stillness the dancing." [11] The mystics express this in another way by saying that God is so bright that He dazzles and blinds the intelligence which is now left in darkness, just as the eyes of the bat are blinded by the sun.

Then there is the All-is-Nothing paradox. When one is in the silence of dark, supraconceptual prayer, one seems to have *nothing* in the mind because all images, concepts, and quiddities have been abandoned. But in fact this apparent nothingness (for here "nothing" is a phenomenological or descriptive word, not to be taken literally) is all, for it is a supraconceptual sense of Being Itself, of Everything, of God.

Similarly there are paradoxes of time and place— "England and nowhere. Never and always." [12] Here it is to be remembered that mystical experience (especially in its highest moments) is enacted outside time and place, a fact attested by John of the Cross and also by the Zennists—"where here and now cease to matter." [13]

And from this it can be seen that for the Dionysian mystics not any paradox will do; there is no question of just playing with words and irrationalities. The paradoxes are based on an accurate, if difficult, metaphysic. Zen, on the other hand, has not yet found a metaphysical basis; nor is it likely to do so if it follows the path traced out by Dr. Suzuki, who has carried the irrational element to its furthest limit. Whereas the Zen masters and Christian mystics declared that it was impossible to say anything about mystical experience, Suzuki seemed to say that it was impossible to say anything about anything. And so he devoted page after page to affirming that it was impossible to affirm and denying that it was possible to deny. It is difficult to absolve the great old man from the charge of taking a

holy delight in mystifying the unenlightened. Moreover it was "Suzuki Zen" which caught on in the West
(his following was much more restricted in Japan)
where he found an audience craving for gnosticism,
glad to escape from reason, dogma, and conceptualism
of any kind. And so the West was deluged with the
torrent of literature he inspired, declaring that left is
right, black is white, and up is down, refusing to make
statements about anything—and asserting that all this
confusion falls beautifully into shape with the advent
of enlightenment. In Japan the Zen masters maintained
their traditional silence; but the West was greatly impressed.

V

In Japan, however, attempts are being made to find a
Zen metaphysics by a group of scholars who are normally not associated with Zen and are scarcely known
by the Zen enthusiasts in the West. I refer to some
Kyoto philosophers inspired by Kitarō Nishida. On
reading his works, one's first impression is of a completely European philosophy filled with quotations from
all the masters from Aristotle to Hegel and from Plotinus to Kant; but a more careful perusal shows that
the fundamental inspiration of all is Zen. "I am not a
psychologist nor a sociologist," he wrote in his diary;
"I shall be an investigator of life. Zen is music, Zen is
art, Zen is movement; apart from this there is nothing
wherein one must seek consolation of the heart. If my
heart can become simple like that of a child, I think
there probably can be no greater happiness than this.
Non multa sed multum." [14] And the mystical flavor of
these words extends itself to the whole life of the great
thinker. In his diary, however, he goes so far as to suggest that he would like to express Zen in a modern theory: "It would be good if after achieving *satori* in one
great truth, one could explain it to others in a modern
theory." But it is as though these words slipped un-

wittingly from his pen; for he later adds: "I was mistaken to use Zen for the sake of scholarship. I should have used it for the spirit and soul. . . ." [15] And yet this desire, rejected as contrary to the whole Zen tradition, greatly influenced his philosophical development.

That Zen is at the root of Nishida's thought can be seen from his incessant preoccupation with experience beyond subject and object, a problem which has intrigued him since the time of his early *A Study of Good*; one gets the impression that he is looking for a rational basis to enlightenment. Recent Japanese writers have pointed out that Nishida was attempting to explain Zen to the West; one cannot but ask if he were also attempting to explain Zen to himself.

It is not my intention here to enter into Nishida's difficult thought, but simply to say that his basic attitude toward enlightenment is not unlike that of the Christian mystical theologian. That is to say, while retaining faith in reason he always comes to a point beyond which the discursive intellect cannot go. And this is mystical experience, transcending words and concepts and syllogisms—something quite inexpressible. In short, we come back to the distinction between knowledge that *transcends,* and that which *contradicts,* reason, realizing that in order to enter the lofty realm of superthinking one may abandon ordinary thinking, one may disparage its tiny light as that of a candle beside the sun; but one need not radically refuse to affirm and deny. The mind working through logic may not know much; but it knows something.

The work of Nishida is continued by his disciples; and it is not impossible that some day a philosophy of Zen may gradually make its appearance.[16]

VI

To put the matter in the terminology I have already used: in all this matter it is possible to distinguish broadly between two types of thinking—one which I

have called "vertical," because in it the mind goes
down; the other "horizontal," because in it images and
ideas pass across the surface of the mind. Vertical thinking is existential in that it does away with differences,
distinctions, quiddities, and essences in order to find the
unity of all things. This is mysticism. The second kind
of thinking, which I have called horizontal, is found
when the mind, preoccupied principally with the stream
of consciousness passing before it, is taken up with diversity rather than with unity—hence it stresses essences, quiddities, differences. Vertical or existential
thinking concentrates on the fact *that* things are, seeing
the unity of all being: horizontal or essential thinking
concentrates on *what* things are, seeing their diversity.
Existential thinking is of a deeper nature (that is why
I have called it vertical), because to see unity one must
go right into reality, bypassing essences—hence it can
be called superthinking or supraconceptual thinking.
On the other hand, essential thinking, though much
wider in scope, remains on the surface of the mind.

Though generalizations are always dangerous, it is
probably true to say that Oriental culture tends to be
existential; in this sense the old cliché about the "mystic East" is not without foundation. In Japan, for instance, the tea ceremony, the flower arrangement, archery, and the rest keep stressing a vertical attitude of
mind—penetration of the object, union with it, forget-
fulness of self, no past or future but only the present
moment. And in keeping with this (or perhaps at the
root of all this) is Zen. Western thought, on the other
hand, until recently has tended to be essential and syllogistic, creating an atmosphere in which the mystics
have not found wholehearted acceptance.

My point here is that both kinds of thinking are necessary, that everyone can gain from a union of the vertical and the horizontal, that both elements must be
found in any future world-culture.

VII

I am aware that what I have written here will be scornfully rejected by certain advocates of Zen who persistently oppose any kind of logic; but I would simply like to reiterate that I am not saying that mystical experience can be explained in words (I have tried to show the contrary), nor even that Nishida's ideal of explaining Zen in a modern theory is possible. What I want to say is that there should be harmony between mystical knowledge and that right reason which it transcends. For, if discursive reasoning is utterly rejected, there is no check, no norm for distinguishing the true mysticism from the false; and history is there to show us that mysticism left unchecked can lead to all sorts of aberrations from waste of time to violent eroticism. In the Christian tradition, mysticism began as a phenomenon or experience (as it appears in the Bible in the case of Moses and St. Paul; and later in the Fathers of the desert), but it was found necessary to give it a philosophical basis—not to explain it but to protect and to guide the mystic through the labyrinthine path lest he fall into the quagmire of absurdity.

And Zen, too, has been protected from error until now by a solid body of practical teaching transmitted from master to disciple through the centuries. But I believe that the time has come to reflect philosophically on this teaching, to see what the paradoxes mean, to examine the relationship of the whole process to reasoning. The result will be that (as in Christian mysticism) many things will remain enigmatic and mysterious to the uninitiated; but the process itself will be strengthened and it will develop.

NOTES

1. Dumoulin, *History of Zen Buddhism*, p. 209.
2. Miura and Sasaki, *Zen Kōan*, p. 50.

3. *Ibid.*, p. 55.
4. *Ibid.*, p. 49.
5. *Ibid.*, p. 52.
6. T. S. Eliot, *East Coker*, lines 138 ff.
7. Koestler, *Lotus*, p. 238.
8. Miura and Sasaki, *Zen Kōan*, p. 47.
9. See *The Epistle of Privy Counsel*, Ch. 1: "And therefore think of God in this work as thou dost on thyself, and on thyself as thou dost on God: that he is as he is and thou art as thou art, so that thy thought be not scattered nor separated, but oned in him that is all."
10. Hakuun, *Kyūdō*, II, p. 14.
11. Eliot, *East Coker*, line 128.
12. T. S. Eliot, *Little Gidding*, line 53.
13. "This prayer, therefore, seems to the soul extremely brief, although, as we may say, it may last for a long period; for the soul has been united in pure intelligence, which belongs not to time; and this is the brief prayer which is said to pierce the heavens, because it is brief and because it belongs not to time" (*Ascent of Mount Carmel*, 11, XIV, ii).
14. See Kitarō Nishida, *A Study of Good*, trans. V. H. Viglielmo (Tokyo, 1960), p. 198.
15. See Lothar Knauth, "Life is Tragic: The Diary of Nishida Kitarō," *Monumenta Nipponica*, 20 (1965).
16. See the work of Shin'ichi Hisamatsu, Keiji Nishitani, and Yoshinori Takeuchi.

6

THE INTUITIVE APPROACH
TO MORALITY

I

One of the most striking features of Zen is its refusal to
create or recognize a scientific ethical system. The masters will say that Zen is beyond good and evil, or they
will emphasize complete liberty of spirit with the counsel: if you want to go, go; if you want to sit, sit; if
you are hungry, eat; if you are sleepy, sleep; and so on.
Thus liberated from burdensome laws, one acts in obedience to one's true self. Hui-neng tells us:

> The person who sees into his True Nature is free
> when he stands as well as when he does not stand.
> He is free both in going and in coming. There is
> nothing which retards him, nothing which hinders
> him. Responding to the situation, he acts accordingly;
> responding to the words, he answers accordingly. He
> expresses himself taking on all forms but he is never
> removed from his Self-Nature.[1]

Here, of course, the key words are "the person who
sees into his True Nature"; for Hui-neng is not saying
that everyone can act with such liberty. But he speaks
for a way of thinking that is deeply embedded in Eastern thought and is closely connected with the Taoist
idea that the good man is the "non-dependent man of
Tao," the man who is spontaneously obedient to
Heaven, the one who acts in accordance with the desires of the heart without breaking the law.

True to this spirit, Nishida places the highest point

of morality, not in thinking and reasoning and fidelity
to law, but in the spontaneous doing of good—which,
however, is only possible when one has reached the Zen
situation beyond subject and object. "Only when subject and object are mutually forgotten and one arrives
at a state wherein there is only the activity of a single
reality in heaven and earth, does one first attain to the
consummation of good behavior." [2]

Something analogous (though not precisely the
same) is found in the Christian life and expressed by
Augustine in his famous dictum "Love and do what
you will"; as if to say that the man who really loves
God and his neighbor need not be anxious about rules
and regulations, since the light of love will spontaneously lead him to do what is right in complete liberty
of spirit. Aquinas, too, speaks of the knowledge of connaturality: love gives a kind of knowledge that is above
all reasoning, a spontaneous intuition of what is right.
Other medieval writers speak of charity as a candle
that illumines all things and shows a person what is to
be done with intuitive accuracy. And Christian writers
speak of the author of this love as the Holy Spirit, who
thus guides His own, teaching them what to do, inspiring them with a divine knowledge of what is right
in the concrete, existential situation. This is the role of
"the living flame of love" that plays so central a part in
the thought of John of the Cross.

Yet the Spirit inspiring this love and wisdom was
never thought of as a "deus ex machina" who guides
men from outside like a driver in an automobile. Fidelity to the Spirit was built on fidelity to one's true nature: the voice of true nature and the voice of the Spirit
speak in such unison that they are barely distinguish-
able. Hence Aquinas can indicate that his own doctrine on this point is rather akin to that of Aristotle.
"Even the Philosopher," he writes, "says in the Chapter on *Good Fortune* that for those moved by divine
instinct, there is no need to take counsel according to
human reason, but only to follow their inner prompt-

ings, since they are moved by a higher than human reason." [3] That is to say, Greek and Christian agree that the ideal of morality is to be found in obedience to a principle beyond rules and regulations.

Obviously this does not mean that St. Thomas despised a science of ethics built on reason. In fact, he devotes a great deal of energy and space to the analysis of the various virtues that go to make up the Christian life; while asserting the superiority of the "divine instinct" and the "inner promptings," he seems to feel that a scientific approach to vice and virtue is a necessary complement. But to preserve the balance between intuition and law has never been easy, and not a few successors of the Angelic Doctor, overlooking his intuitive approach through connaturality, concentrated on cataloguing virtues and vices one by one (seven deadly sins, seven corporal works of mercy, cardinal virtues, theological virtues, and so on), making of solid virtues ideals to be acquired in the building-up of the good man and the acquisition of perfection. This approach was not uninfluenced by Greek ethical writings which extolled the beauty of justice, temperance, friendship, and all those qualities that go to make up Aristotle's "good life" with less emphasis on the "inner promptings." Recent Christian writers, however, tend to criticize this way of thinking as too easily degenerating into casuistry and legalism; the modern existentialist approach prefers to see all virtues as expressions of something deeper—namely, a fundamental choice, a direction in life, a basic love of God.

Be that as it may, the Christian approach to prayer was greatly influenced by the approach to virtue. Prayer, besides being an encounter with God, was looked upon as a means for the acquisition of virtue. Especially in that kind of mental prayer that came to be associated with the name of Ignatius of Loyola, one reflected on the value and necessity of the virtues, resolving to put them into practice; or one meditated on the virtues of Christ with the determination to imitate them. Thus prayer was a road to virtue; and progress in virtue was the norm of the genuineness of prayer.

But then there was mystical prayer. Here, there was obviously no reflection on virtues, even on the virtues of Christ in His historical life; for the mind, emptied of thoughts and images of all kinds, remained rapt in supraconceptual silence. But yet mystical prayer, far from being divorced from virtue, was the supreme road thereto. Teresa of Avila never tires of emphasizing that, as one descends into successive mansions, virtues are rooted ever more deeply in the personality and practiced with increasing ease. Even though one never thinks about virtues, they are implanted in a wonderful way. Without thinking about poverty, one becomes poor in spirit; without reflecting on humility, one becomes humble; without touching on the subject of prudence, one becomes prudent. "There is no necessity for going about searching for reasons on the strength of which we may elicit acts of humility and of shame," writes St. Teresa for those enjoying the prayer of quiet, "because Our Lord Himself supplies them in a way very different from that by which we could acquire them." And all the old spiritual authorities kept insisting that the only sure test of a healthy mystical life was growth in solid virtue. Where this was absent, silent prayer might be no more than idle dreaming.

Some mystical writers went further. They declared that there were certain virtues that can *only* be acquired in the passivity of mystical prayer. Speaking of the weakness of beginners, John of the Cross, after distinguishing two kinds of defects, goes on to assert that "neither from these imperfections nor from those others can the soul be perfectly purified until God brings it into the passive purgation of that dark night whereof we shall speak presently." [4] And the author of *The Cloud of Unknowing*, too, follows the traditional doctrine that, whereas discursive prayer removes defects, mystical prayer removes the *roots* of these defects—by which he means concupiscence arising from original sin.

In short, both mystical writers see that this kind of prayer is influencing the psychic life at a much deeper level than would discursive prayer. This latter remains on the surface of the psychic life; mystical prayer goes deep, and the virtues it implants spring so spontaneously from the inner core of one's being that they are practiced with ease.

Now, in Zen some parallels can be observed. Japanese thought has less of the Greek cataloguing of virtues and vices. Though there were some virtues (detachment, poverty, endurance, and patience in adversity) that the ancients loved and admired, the idea of pondering on them and praying God to inculcate them is not found in Japan. Yet the masters, after practising their silent Zen, turned out good, virtuous men, as anyone who has met them will testify. That is to say, they emptied the mind of thoughts and concepts, remained in silent emptiness, and this tranquil passivity gave birth to deep virtue.

The problem therefore arises how this mystical silence is connected with the acquisition of virtue; one cannot but wonder where these virtues come from and how the silence of mystical prayer implants them so deeply in the mind. Modern people cannot be satisfied with the answer that God simply "gives" virtue to the mystic like a "deus ex machina"; they want to see the secondary cause; they want to see an intrinsic connection between the silent depths of contemplative prayer and the virtue it implants in the soul. I would like here to give a tentative solution to this problem.

II

Anyone who has read the mystics knows immediately that a word constantly on their lips is "detachment." To advance along the mystical path, detachment is a condition as well as a goal. Moreover, the passive and silent Zen concentration with its withdrawal of all the faculties into the core of one's being has the effect of

severing the ties which bind one to surrounding exter-
nals. And so is effected a serenity and a liberation stemming from a species of isolation or solitude. This condition of detachment will grow and grow as one descends
deeper and deeper into the caverns of one's own mind,
getting away from the outside world. It is one of the
outstanding characteristics in the personality of a true
Zen monk, and it is reflected in the calm composure of
so much Buddhist art.

In John of the Cross, too, the "nothing, nothing,
nothing" that fills his pages means the most rigorous
detachment from all things, be they material or spiritual, natural or supernatural—it entails detachment
from the most basic need of man: the need of knowledge, concepts, reasoning; it asks the giving up of consolations in prayer, visions, ecstasies, or whatever it
may be. In the *Ascent* the active effort at detachment
is underlined: in *The Dark Night* we are told how the
very fact of silent, supraconceptual prayer in love
achieves automatically a deep serenity in the annihila-
tion of the most deep-rooted desires. The author of *The
Cloud of Unknowing* outlines his doctrine of detachment in a different way by saying that man, "scattered"
by original sin, is poured out over created things; but
by contemplation he is gradually torn away from crea-
tures and unified within himself so that all his faculties
are fixed on God who is the true Being of all that is.
Here it is apparent (and of supreme importance) that
for the Christian mystics detachment is a path of another kind: it is a path to love.

But as far as detachment is concerned, it is probable
that the silent, supraconceptual concentration of Zen
and the "living flame of love" of Christian mystics
achieve a somewhat similar effect, withdrawing desires
from objects to which they are inordinately drawn. It
is true, of course, that one can be in some measure detached from created things without devoting oneself to
Zen or Christian mystical prayer, but the kind of detachment stemming from reasoning, thinking, and the

exercising of the will always remains at a superficial level of the psychic life; nor does it develop into that virtue practised with ease which St. Thomas desires and which one associates with both Christian perfection and the state of Nirvana. It is precisely the silent absence of concepts and thinking, found in both Zen and Christian mysticism, that produces a condition of calm and rigorous detachment peculiarly its own. The point at issue, then, is this: is this mystical detachment something so radical that it can produce all other virtues?

III

That detachment—which at first sight seems a cold and inhuman virtue—is in fact of primary importance for normal human development, is an ordinary finding of modern psychology, which insists that one can find balanced emotional maturity only by a process of detachment's extending its roots into the subliminal regions of the psyche and eliminating subconscious fixations acquired in earlier periods of life. Erich Fromm tells us that detachment is something so vitally linked to human growth that it must begin at the moment of birth and proceed over one's whole life—which, when all goes well, is nothing more than growth through a series of crises. "The aim of life," he writes, "is to be fully born"; and he goes on to say that some people "cannot cut the umbilical cord completely, as it were; they remain symbiotically attached to mother, father, family, race, state, status, money, gods, etc.; they never emerge fully as themselves and thus they never become fully born." [5] Here from a psychologist is a program of detachment as ruthless as that of John of the Cross, showing that the human perfection aimed at by the psychologist is not alien to the Christian perfection of the saints. Indeed, John of the Cross uses words reminiscent of those I have quoted from Fromm, for he complains that some people, retarded in their spiritual

life "still think of God as little children and speak of
God as little children, and feel and experience God as
little children." [6] In other words, he wants people to
get rid of children's ideas of God and to grow up. It is
of interest to note, also, that the detachment demanded
in both cases is one that influences subliminal regions
of the mind; it is a kind of detachment which cannot be
attained to simply by strength of will and a determination to break the tie binding one to the thing one loves.
In order to attain to the fullness of human perfection it
is necessary that certain regions of one's unconscious
mind be purified; and this is done by mystical experience and perhaps it is also done by psychoanalysis. This
indeed seems to be one of the main points of *The Cocktail Party*, in which the spiritual director, Harcourt-
Reilly, is also a psychoanalyst and guides his subjects
through a quasi-mystical purification of the unconscious.

Dr. Fromm carries his program of detachment to its
furthermost limits; for he finally asserts that man should
even be detached from the illusion of a fatherly God.
"If man gives up his illusion of a fatherly God," he
writes, "if he faces his aloneness and insignificance in
the universe, he will be like a child that has left his
father's house. But it is the very aim of human development to overcome this infantile fixation." [7]

To the Christian these words might at first sound
blasphemous; and it is true that no convinced believer
in the Bible would express the thing in this way. Yet I
believe that Dr. Fromm's words are open to a Christian
interpretation: I should like to think that he means, not
that man should be detached from God (who is his
very being and the source of all that is), but that he
can (and at the height of mystical experience should)
be detached from *images and concepts of God*. For,
once again, the "nothing, nothing, nothing" of John of
the Cross includes precisely this sweeping-away of images and thoughts of God to meet Him in the darkness
and obscurity of pure faith which is above all con-

cepts. Images may lead to an anthropomorphic notion of God unless one is sufficiently detached from them to see that they contain an element of falsehood. Concretely, if when calling God a father I include in this notion the characteristics of an earthly father and apply them to God univocally, then my notion of God becomes anthropomorphic, and it is, as Dr. Fromm says, the "illusion of a fatherly God." In fact, when the mystics come face-to-face with God, He is like a wall of nothingness: He is the mystery of mysteries; He is, as St. John of the Cross says, like night to the soul. For He transcends all thoughts and concepts.

Growth, then, demands detachment; and both growth and detachment are difficult for man. Psychologists who think like Fromm will say that it is precisely the refusal to accept the fact of growth that causes complexes, psychological retardations, and neuroses. For human nature shrinks from growth just as the child is reluctant to leave its mother's womb and its mother's breast, and as the adolescent shrinks from the unknown adult world that rises before him. For psychological growth is a journey into unknown territory; and no one likes to leave the drab Platonic cave where he sits in sad security. Hence, man must muster all his psychological force to overcome each crisis and to avoid slipping back into infantilism.

If one does not succeed in growing through detachment, the result is retardation, infantilism, and, at the extreme stage, neurosis. And it is interesting to see how modern Christian ascetical literature, influenced by this way of thinking, links moral virtue to psychic growth. The old terminology that spoke of static virtues is fast disappearing in favor of a way of speaking more in keeping with depth psychology. Whereas previously people spoke of their predominant fault as vanity or selfishness or whatever it might be, and made as their aim the acquisition of solid virtues such as humility and charity, the modern tendency is to speak of virtue and vice in terms of growth. Thus, for example, faults

of a certain character, sin, crime will be attributed
to a compensatory urge to make up for a deep-seated
sense of insecurity caused in the child deprived of
love or loved too much. Or difficulties in obedience
(which might formerly have been attributed to pride)
may be ascribed to a latent hatred of one's father—
and there are fixations, fears of parents, and so on
which have never been outgrown. Or, again, temptation, in the light of psychoanalysis, may often be attributed to an urge to return to the psychic life of
childhood.

In short, the great triumph of psychoanalysis is to
have found the roots of vices and temptations and to
have discovered that (in many cases, at any rate) they
are frustrations arising from early psychic crises never
fully overcome; that is why modern ascetical literature
speaks of the great virtue as being "emotional maturity." This means that, in order to acquire moral
virtue, one must grow. Even in the overcoming of defects, modern psychologists will hold that it is often
better not to concentrate on this or that particular defect, but rather to ensure that the personality as a
whole develops and grows in such a way that the defect will naturally disappear. For example, uncontrollable outbursts of anger may be better overcome by a
development of the whole personality than by resolu-
tions that "I will not be angry," repeated at fixed in-
tervals (though this also may, of course, be one way
to self-control). But the point is that the defect may
be an expression of some lack of growth in a deeper
sector of the psyche.

IV

From this it can be seen that often the root of defects
and of vice is latent, alive in the unconscious realm of
the mind. In order that true virtue may be acquired,
it is necessary to purify not only the conscious regions
but also those deeper regions where the roots are situ-

ated. And mysticism does precisely this, producing its effect in the subliminal part of the mind which is normally dormant, uncovering motives that are ordinarily submerged, making an impact on that part of the mind which is also touched by psychoanalysis. At the beginning of *The Dark Night of the Soul*, St. John of the Cross makes a devastating analysis of the faults of beginners (following the line of the seven deadly sins), showing that the beginner in the spiritual life is in reality constantly deceiving himself. Whereas he thinks he is seeking God, he is in fact seeking his own consolation; whereas he thinks he is virtuous, he is full of vanity. Which is to say in modern parlance: his real is different from his conscious motivation. And then the Spanish saint goes on to say that only by the dark night of mystical contemplation can this unconscious motivation be purified. It is interesting again to compare all this with the words of Erich Fromm:

> Psychoanalysis has given the concept of truth a new dimension. In pre-analytic thinking a person could be considered to speak the truth if he believed in what he was saying. Psychoanalysis has shown that subjective conviction is by no means a sufficient criterion of sincerity. A person can believe that he acts out of a sense of justice and yet be motivated by cruelty. He can believe that he is motivated by love and yet be driven by a craving for masochistic dependence. A person can believe that duty is his guide though his main motivation is vanity.[8]

John of the Cross lived in the time of "pre-analytic thinking," but I believe he saw the truth of what Dr. Fromm here says (except, of course, that he would deny "that subjective conviction is by no means a sufficient criterion of sincerity," for no man can be held fully responsible for unconscious motives over which he has little control)—but he would (and does) say that for the fullness of Christian perfection this unconscious region of the mind must also be purified. And he asserts that it is in fact purified by mystical prayer, which thus is the way, and the only way, to implant virtue in the deepest part of the soul.

V

On the other hand, to keep describing man's life as a growing detachment, as a series of ruptures with other things and persons, as a constant breaking, breaking, breaking away—this alone is negative; it leaves us dangling helplessly over the appalling abyss of isolation and alienation that fills the pages of so much modern literature. It is true, of course, that the life of man and the life of the mystic (which is no more than a deeply human life) has this aspect; and the mystic often comes up against the wall of nothingness, of blackness, of the void to which Fromm also seems to lead. But this is only one aspect.

In fact, detachment is only a means to attachment: it is the means to the establishment of a new, a wider, a deeper relationship. Thus, when the umbilical cord is cut (to come back to Fromm's example), the child breaks with the body of its mother to establish a new and wider relationship with the family; at adolescence he breaks with his family for a wider relationship with the outside world; the celibate man or woman gives up the exclusive relationship with a marriage partner for a wider relationship with all men and with God; and so on. That is to say, the severing of a relationship in detachment can be justified only by the creation of a new and deeper relationship. And this deeper relationship with all men and with God can be called emotional maturity or humility or what-you-will. But it is some form of love. "Analytic therapy," writes Fromm again, "is essentially an attempt to help the patient gain or regain his capacity for love. If this aim is not fulfilled nothing but surface changes can be accomplished." [9]

Indeed, neither Zen nor Christian mysticism could be justified, if they were simply a cutting-off of self from all things. That Christian mysticism, far from being so, is a way to love is clear enough from the protests of St. John of the Cross that all his doctrine of detachment is no more than a means to the practice of the First Commandment to love God with all one's heart and soul; and, as I have already said, the detachment of *The Cloud of Unknowing* is simply a means to fix the faculties on God. In Zen, as in Buddhism generally, the element of positive love is less conspicuous; but that it is not completely absent is clear from the gratitude and kindness of those who have persevered to the peak-point of *satori*. T. S. Eliot, who exposes a Christian apophatic mysticism with some Buddhist influence, beautifully puts together the stillness of detachment and progress in unitive love when he writes:

> We must be still and still moving
> Into another intensity
> For a further union, a deeper communion.[10]

That is to say, the stillness of silent prayer is leading to a more intense union with God and man, to a deeper love. Now to answer the question posed at the beginning.

The silence of mysticism implants virtues in the soul precisely because it effects a certain deep detachment which, in turn, leads to love. And that one who loves has all the virtues is stated again and again in the scriptures: in the last analysis there is not a multiplicity of virtues but only one virtue. From modern psychology we find Erich Fromm asserting that love is the peakpoint of emotional maturity.

At the same time I would like to point out that I here speak of the moral aspect of Christian love. For it is quite possible that a person with a deep neurosis, incapable of a full love in the moral sense, and greatly oriented towards immorality, may at the same time be filled with Christian charity—though this would not appear on the surface but only in his heroic efforts

to please God. But such persons (whom I like to call
the Graham Greene saints) even though their merit
may be great can scarcely be said to possess Christian
love in the full sense. For true virtue (to return to
Aquinas) should be practiced with ease.

VI

Returning now to the whole question of interior liberty
and fidelity to oneself or to the promptings of the Holy
Spirit, it is clear that if through silent detachment one
is cleansed of interior impurity it is enough to be
obedient to the inner light; for a great deal of virtue
is planted so firmly in the deepest realm of the psyche
that it guides one spontaneously in the path of love.
The point is, however, that such spontaneous virtue is
only possible after years and years of efforts at detachment through a life lived faithfully according to ethical
norms. Confucius claimed to have reached this stage
at the age of seventy; and in the Christian tradition
no one is advised to lean completely on his inner inspirations until his interior, even his mystical, life is
highly developed.

Indeed, this was precisely one of the main points at
issue at the time of the Reformation, when the Re-
formers stood strongly in favor of the inner light while
Catholics put their emphasis on external authority.
The battle between these two ways of thought raged
for a long time, with men like Chesterton ridiculing
what he called FIF (funny interior feeling) and remarking that when Jones obeys the inner light, Jones
obeys Jones. Yet Catholic theologians will now admit
that the Catholic position was overdone and that personal responsibility was sacrificed to legalism. Church
unity is helping to bring about harmony between fidelity to one's inner promptings and obedience to external law, but the fact still remains that to put emphasis exclusively on the inner promptings of the spirit
cannot be the solution for the vast majority of people.

This is because the heart of man, unless prepared by many years of the good life, is filled with all sorts of promptings; and it is virtually impossible to distinguish between one's truest self and other nondescript, or even dangerous, promptings that rise up from the depths of one's unconscious. In some of his most powerful passages, Jung well describes the inner prompting, which he calls "vocation," that arises dynamically in the heart of man. This vocation he describes as "an irrational factor that destines a man to emancipate himself from the herd and from its well-worn paths." And he continues:

> But vocation acts like a law of God from which there is no escape. The fact that many a man who goes his own way ends in ruin means nothing to one who has a vocation. He *must* obey his own law, as if it were a daemon whispering to him of new and wonderful paths. Anyone with a vocation hears the voice of the inner man: he is *called*. That is why the legends say that he possesses a private daemon who counsels him and whose mandates he must obey.[11]

Such a vocation, however, may not be the voice of the Spirit; it may not be the prompting of one's true self; it may be the voice of a dangerous neurosis. And recent history has taught the world the terrible danger of the man with a vocation, the fanatic who must obey his inner voice in the way Jung here describes. Jung himself would seem to support this from another passage where he remarks:

> Generally speaking, all the life which the parents could have lived, but of which they thwarted themselves for artificial motives, is passed on to the children in substitute form. That is to say, the children are driven unconsciously in a direction that is intended to compensate for everything that was left unfulfilled in the lives of their parents.[12]

All this proves clearly enough that the utmost prudence is required to decide whether an inner prompting is

the voice of one's true self or the neurotic voice of an
unfulfilled desire communicated from one's parents or
the voice of a compensatory inferiority complex or
whatever it may be.

And because of this, for all those persons who have
not reached the summit of mystical detachment (and
perhaps even for those who have), a science of ethics
and asceticism is necessary, not to crush their inner
promptings and not to take their place, but to ensure
that they are genuine. This, I believe, is well grasped
by Ignatius of Loyola when in his *Spiritual Exercises*
he leads the exercitant to make a decision. Following
the tradition of the Church, he wishes that the resolution be taken according to the promptings of the Spirit
(what he calls the second method of election, and in
harmony with what elsewhere he calls "the interior
law of charity and love"); but, far from rejecting ordinary thinking and weighing of reasons, he insists
that one must ponder on the pros and cons—to check
the validity of an experience which is quasi-mystical
but subject to illusion. In this way, he unites reasoning
and intuition, the latter being tested by the former.

VII

The history of religion is filled with examples of people who have fallen into absurdity, deceiving themselves and others, because of fidelity to an inner
prompting. There are few dicta that can be more dis-
astrously abused than the Augustinian one already
quoted, which can easily deviate into "do what you
will" without the "love," thus leading to license. And
in the same way, it is well known that the detachment
attained to in Zen and Yoga has been used to deaden
the moral conscience, thus enabling one to practice
immorality with equilibrium. It is this that makes imperative a system of ethics. On the other hand, morality would always remain cramping and sterile if it
were mere fidelity to a science that propounded ethical

laws of right action. Intuitive obedience to one's truest self, properly understood, is more accurate than reasoning; and the highest morality is surely found in genuine mysticism. For, just as the inner light can be illusory, so can a person deceive himself by discursive thinking. By specious reasons and casuistry, one can rationalize a line of conduct which would never be countenanced if only one were face-to-face with one's truest self and God in complete honesty and naked truth. That is why the two should be united: an exact science of ethics protecting the voice of one's deepest self.

It is to the everlasting credit of Zen to have found a technique for attaining detachment which the West never knew. The silent, cross-legged sitting is a powerful way to virtue, to an intuitive morality, and to that "indifference" which is the basis of an ethical life. But a scientific ethical system, built upon a clear metaphysics, could only help Zen, destroying nothing of its love of inner freedom. The two approaches, which we may loosely call Eastern and Western, can complement and help each other.

NOTES

1. See Shin'ichi Hisamatsu, "The Character of Oriental Nothingness," *Philosophical Studies of Japan*, II (1960), pp. 65 ff.
2. Nishida, *Study of Good*.
3. *Summa theol.* 1a 2ae, q. 68 a. 1.
4. John of the Cross, *Dark Night*, Bk. I, Ch. III.
5. Erich Fromm, *Psychoanalysis and Religion* (New Haven, 1963), p. 79.
6. John of the Cross, *Dark Night*, Bk. II, Ch. III.
7. Fromm, *Psychoanalysis and Religion*, p. 13.
8. *Ibid.*, p. 77.
9. *Ibid.*, p. 87.
10. Eliot, *East Coker*, lines 204 ff.
11. Jung, *Development of Personality*, pp. 175–176.
12. *Ibid.*, p. 191.

7

ZEN AND "AMAERU"

I

Recent times have witnessed a good deal of discussion about the East and the West, about what constitutes the "Oriental mind," about the chief ingredient in the Japanese psyche, and so on. It is said that what is peculiarly Japanese is alternately Confucianism or Zen or Shintoism or something which escapes all labels and is simply "Japanese."

Interesting light has been thrown on this problem by a distinguished psychiatrist, Dr. L. Takeo Doi, whose writings have aroused considerable interest both in Japan and in the United States. His approach, of course, is not religious or historical but psychological —somewhat in the line made famous by Ruth Benedict.[1]

Dr. Doi (who bases his theory on his own clinical experience) holds that a key concept for the understanding of the Japanese character is the somewhat baffling word *amaeru*—baffling, that is, for some Westerners but completely intelligible to the smallest Japanese child. It expresses the desire to be loved or to depend emotionally upon another. But perhaps it is better here to let Dr. Doi speak for himself:

Amae is the noun form of *amaeru*, an intransitive verb which means "to depend and presume upon another's benevolence." This word has the same root as *amai*, an adjective which means "sweet." This *amaeru* has a distinct feeling of sweetness, and is generally used to describe a child's attitude or be-

119

havior toward his parents, particularly his mother.
But it can also be used to describe the relationship
between two adults, such as the relationship between
a husband and a wife or a master and a subordinate.
I believe that there is no single word in English
equivalent to *amaeru*. . . .[2]

Elsewhere, Dr. Doi returns to the translation of this
word, saying that it means "to depend and presume
upon another's love," [3] or "to seek and bask in another's
indulgence." [4]

The point to be noted, however, is that it refers
primarily to the mother–child relationship, a relationship which, says Dr. Doi, is prolonged in Japan where
"the dependency of children on parents is fostered
even beyond the nursing period and its behavior pattern is institutionalized into its social structure." [5] In
a series of brilliant studies, Dr. Doi shows how this
desire for emotional dependence expressed by *amaeru*
extends itself to almost every branch of social life in
Japan: it played its role in the prewar Emperor system; it fits in with the *giri* and *ninjō*, which are so
central to all Japanese social and interpersonal relationships.[6] And indeed his theory is rendered plausible
by statements made independently by other psychiatrists to the effect that the mother–child relationship in
Japan is very strong, partly because the father is constantly absent from the home so that the education of
the child is entrusted almost completely to the mother.
If this is so, it is easy to see how an early-established
emotional dependency might continue into later life,
and might even create a social climate which demands
a certain *amaeru* or dependence on the organization
of the company, the school, the religious group, and
so on. Dr. Doi points to two popular sayings which
illustrate his point: "Go under a big tree, if you want
to depend" and "A nail that sticks out will be hit
hard." The first recommends dependency and the second prohibits independence. And so in Japan the indi-

vidual should not strive for independence but should endeavor to efface himself in the crowd.

II

What interests me most, however, are the few scattered remarks made by Dr. Doi about the repercussions of *amaeru* on Japanese religious life. He feels that the urge to seek the Zen enlightenment (the loss of one-self in the totality) is not without relationship to *amaeru*. Here is a passage in which he recapitulates what I have written above and applies it to Zen:

> The dependency wish as expressed by *amaeru* may be defined as "to seek a restoration of the once-lost quasi-union of mother and infant" or, borrowing Freud's term, "to experience the oceanic feeling." It at once attempts to overcome the pain of separation and to deny its reality. In other words, it can be said that one who does *amaeru* presumes upon the one-ness of self and other. For the average person in Japanese society, however, the oneness of self and other is usually only a pretension or at most an illusion shared by the majority of one's group. But some people may be driven to a profound negation, as in Zen Buddhism where one's self is submerged into a Cosmic Self and the identity of subject and object is intuited.[7]

Freud's "oceanic feeling" is the feeling of being inseparably united with the universe; if Dr. Doi's theory is correct, then the person in search of *satori* would (in some cases, at any rate; for there is no need to generalize) be looking for a relationship not unlike that of the mother and child, a relationship in which the self is lost in that greater reality which is now not the mother but the universe or the Cosmic Self. As the child, utterly absorbed in the mother to whom it belongs and of which it is a part, has no personality of its own, so the Zen contemplative has lost his ego in the universe which is all. Hence the *muga*, the *mushin*, the nothingness, the emptiness, the void. It is well known that Dōgen spoke of "anxiety" as the basic drive that impelled men to look for enlightenment; if this theory is true, then this basic anxiety would (in many cases) arise from the frustration of a deeply buried longing to lose oneself in total dependence on the other.

III

Naturally enough, the question arises about Westerners who feel the fascination of the silence of Zen. It is well known that the "Zen boom" in Europe and the United States has not yet entirely passed away; one might ask how this can be accounted for—since Western culture, far from cultivating *amaeru*, emphasizes the independence of the ego, holding out to the world an ideal of personal liberty. To this, Dr. Doi gives another answer. The West, it is true, has always stressed a free and independent ego which is the very antithesis of the Japaneese *amaeru;* but this independence has been overstressed and the lonely ego of Western man finds, in many cases, that it can no longer cope with the situation it has created, and feels an ever-growing insecurity:

> It is known that the West has experienced a great turmoil and confusion, politically as well as culturally, since the beginning of the century. Thus Western people are no more sure of the permanence, if not the rationale, of those values which they have held for centuries. In this predicament, it is interesting, some of them turn to Oriental mysticism, particularly Zen which promises to abolish the appearance of a solitary and anxiety-ridden selfhood alienated from others and the world.[8]

It is this overdeveloped ego, this "solitary and anxiety-ridden selfhood" (so prominent in the existentialists)

which drives some Westerners to the self-forgetfulness of Zen mysticism. "Since the perception of one's
individual separate self is most disturbing," says Dr.
Doi, "it has to be dissolved in the feeling of unity
with one's surroundings or with nature. *Perhaps I
should say 'with Mother Nature,' which is more meaningful psychoanalytically.*" [9] I italicize these latter
words because they indicate that even in the Western
pursuit of Zen the *amaeru* search for the mother–child
relationship is not completely absent.

In short, this would indicate that the longing for
silence, the hankering for passivity, the love of solitude, the world, the submerging of self—all this may
originate in the desire for dependence, total dependence like that of the child on its mother. It explains
why Zen should be deeply engraved in the Japanese
psyche (where the need of *amaeru* is strong) but it
also acknowledges that certain Westerners, shrinking
from the insecurity of an exaggerated freedom, should
long for a similar dependence.

IV

Now, in his exposition of the theory which I have
tried to outline, Dr. Doi scrupulously avoids making
any judgments about the value of Zazen. He never
says, for example, that it is a regression to childhood;
neither does he say that it is the true answer to the
problem of dependence, a problem felt deeply both
in the East and in the West. He simply exposes his
scientific theory. Perhaps he prefers to leave the value
judgment to those whose business is religion, and for
this reason I should like to discuss it a little more here.

At first sight it might seem that he has loaded the
dice heavily against Zen. Yet, some more consideration
of the matter has led me to believe that this is not so,
and that one can hold that the Zen experience is very
meaningful without discounting anything that he says.
Let me explain.

If the theory of Dr. Doi is true, then Zen is often an attempt to solve *the need of dependence*—a need which is basically human and universal, albeit some feel it more deeply than others; for the need to depend is not in itself something abnormal. Everyone must depend on something. The child's *amaeru* feeling is completely normal: so much so that the child which did not want to bask in the indulgent love of its mother would be a strange freak—it cannot but long for the maternal care.

To say, then, that an adult should not have a childish *amaeru* dependence is not to say that he should be utterly independent. On the contrary, he should depend on something; he should acknowledge his human weakness; if he proclaims himself utterly independent he tells a lie. And, in fact, most honest people will admit that they depend on money or success or reputation or status or work or whatever it may be—things that are ultimately no more than drugs. As for religious people, they will admit that they ought to depend on God, independence from whom would be the height of pride. In other words, the whole problem is not whether or not one is dependent, but on what one depends, since in the last analysis no one is independent. And in the case of religious people there is the added problem of the manner of their dependence (for they will admit that their dependence on God should not, psychologically speaking, be the same as that of the person who depends on the aforesaid drugs).

The Zennist, contrary to Christian or other religious people, does not profess any dependence on a deity. Rather does he believe that he liberates himself from dependence of any kind by a rigorous program of detachment from all things, spiritual and material. He has even tried to detach himself from thinking and reasoning, so that absolutely nothing is left on which to rely. Then in the moment of enlightenment he reaches the goal, abandons his anguish, and finds something ultimate which he calls the Cosmic Self or Nothing or

All—or which (more correctly) he refuses to define at all because it is inexpressible in words. But I wonder if what he has reached in *satori* is a pure consciousness of dependence (or a consciousness of pure dependence) without a knowledge of what is depended upon. If one were to say that the Zen contemplative is, in the last analysis, looking for what Christians call God, most Zen people would reject outright this way of speaking. Yet one cannot but wonder if they are not seeking something upon which it is impossible to put any name except that of God. For the Christian God is the mystery of mysteries, the inexpressible. He is All and Nothing; one meets Him in the void. He transcends all designations because (as Aquinas says) whatever concept we may use, God escapes it by reason of His pre-eminence. The Christian mystics often speak of God in terms very reminiscent of Zen; they, too, disclaim dependence upon anything material or spiritual except Something ineffable that can only be grasped in the nothingness and the night of faith. Perhaps they, too, attain to a consciousness of pure dependence; and only dark faith gives them the knowledge that what they depend upon is the transcendent God who can only be "known by unknowing," who can be loved but not known.

Be that as it may, Zen seems to provide some kind of solution to a problem which is universal: on what must I depend? That the type of person who feels this problem most keenly is precisely the one who has had a strong childish dependence on the mother is not impossible. To acknowledge this is not to condemn Zen or to detract from its value. Yet it would have to be maintained that such persons are not the only ones who feel the fascination of Zen. Undoubtedly there are other kinds of persons, other kinds of motivation: it would take an enormous retrospective study to prove that the great Zen contemplatives had a fixation regarding their infant *amaeru*. But that some of them were thus motivated is quite credible.

V

Moreover, it is interesting to note that in certain forms of Christian mysticism the ego, too, is lost or forgotten in the great ocean which is God. This tendency to forget one's own being in the ecstatic consciousness of the All is particularly marked in the Rhineland mystics, in the author of *The Cloud of Unknowing*, and in that whole mystical stream which is called apophatic or Dionysian. Nor is it at all impossible that here, too, the mystic was initially motivated by a desire to depend on something ultimate rather than on the ersatz and drugs that he saw around him. If so, he was seeking (and finding) the solution to a problem that is universal.

Furthermore, it is not impossible that in some cases his motivation may have been connected with something akin to *amaeru*. He may well have been the kind of man who felt this problem very keenly because of a protracted dependence on the mother in childhood. I say "may have been" because there could never be sufficient evidence to assert that it was indeed so. What can be said, however, is that there was (and is) a mystical temperament which may well be bound up with certain factors in childhood. It is precisely because they have realized this that Christian spiritual directors have been wary about mystical people and have always argued that the love of silence, solitude, and self-forgetfulness must be curbed and controlled. On the other hand, the fact that a mystical temperament in a given case stems from a childish *amaeru* is not in itself a reason for checking its tendencies, though it might call for prudence and caution in the directing of such people. At any rate, the existence of a mystical temperament cannot be denied; and in many cases it may be the result of such factors as Dr. Doi has outlined.

VI

In a fairly recent observation, Dr. Doi asserts that the changed conditions of postwar Japanese society are creating a psychological crisis which cries for a solution:

> At any rate, the post-war trend has made one crucial conflict manifest, that is, the conflict over *amaeru* or that of whether one is loved or not. I say this conflict is crucial because one's self-respect in the final analysis hinges upon its successful solution. Only when one is certain on this score is one able to stand as an independent individual.[10]

So the problem comes down to the most basic need in human nature: the need to be loved. The old Japanese society at least provided a framework to take care of this need—or, rather, to check the conflict resulting from it. But Dr. Doi asks what can do this work now, and how the problem can be solved today. "Would it be," he asks, "by acquiring the inner certainty of being loved once for all, or by dispensing with dependency wishes altogether?" This is indeed an interesting question, and it raises the further one whether the inner certainty of being loved once for all can be acquired.

It is tempting to say that true Christian faith provides such certainty by its assurance of God's immense love. Yet I cannot confidently assert this. I myself believe that the inner certainty of being loved once for all can never be completely acquired existentially—and this precisely constitutes the inescapable anguish of man in his earthly pilgrimage. He may, of course, know by faith that God loves him once for all; and he may believe this with all his being. But faith is faith: it is not vision; it is "dark"; it inevitably contains what theologians now call the "element of risk." Faith accompanied by hope gives as much assurance as is possible; but the inner certainty of being loved once for all, together with its perfect security, is not accorded to man in this life. Indeed, we know that not infrequently people with deep, even heroic, faith have suffered acutely from a sense of guilt, of abandonment, of not being loved at all.

On the other hand the experience of the Zen people and the Christian apophatic mystics does seem to offer some solution to the problem of dependence by eliminating reliance on what I have called drugs in favor of dependence on something ultimate. This is not dispensing with dependency wishes altogether but finding the truest meaning of human dependence. Perhaps it is because they do this that both Zen and Christian mysticism are often called therapeutic.

NOTES

1. Dr. Doi is Psychiatrist-in-Chief, St. Luke's International Hospital, Tokyo, and Lecturer, University of Tokyo.
2. L. Takeo Doi, "Amae—A Key Concept for Understanding Japanese Personality Structure," *Psychologia*, 5 (1962), p. 1; the same study is also to be found in Robert J. Smith and Richard K. Beardsley, eds., *Japanese Culture: Its Development and Characteristics* (Chicago, 1962).
3. Doi, "Morita Therapy," p. 120.
4. L. Takeo Doi, "Giri-Ninjō: An Interpretation," *Psychologia,* (1966), p. 7.
5. Doi, "Psychoanalytic Therapy."
6. Doi, "Giri-Ninjō," pp. 8–11.
7. Doi, "Psychoanalytic Therapy."
8. *Ibid.*
9. Doi, "Morita Therapy," p. 121.
10. Doi, "Giri-Ninjō," p. 11.

8

DEFINING MYSTICISM

I have said a good deal about "mysticism" without attempting to define the word. This was not by accident. So much controversy and confusion surrounds this problem that it seemed better to begin by making clear the state of the question with concrete examples. Now, however, it is time to make clear what mysticism is; but before doing so I would like to point to its role (taken in the popular sense) in Buddhism and Christianity.

I

Buddhism is essentially a mystical religion in the popular sense of the word, not only because it originates with the enlightenment of the Buddha, but also because its whole doctrine is focused upon a re-enactment in one's life of this liberating experience of the founder. For this reason it is sometimes said that Zen is the purest form of Buddhism, since its whole meaning is summed up in *satori*. "At all events," writes Dr. Suzuki, "there is no Zen without *satori*, which is indeed the Alpha and Omega of Zen Buddhism. Zen devoid of *satori* is like a sun without its light and heat. Zen may lose its literature, all its monasteries, and all its paraphernalia; but as long as there is *satori* in it, it will survive to eternity." [1] In this way, *satori* (which, for the moment, I shall presume to call "mystical") is the very kernel of Zen Buddhism; and others after Suzuki continue to stress that *kenshō* or "seeing into the essence of things" is the all-important thing for the Zen monk. Daito Kokushi, founder of the

temple of Daitoku-ji, in his last sermon makes an ad-
monition that is typical:

> Some of you may preside over large and flourishing
> temples with Buddha-shrines and rolls of scripture
> gorgeously decorated with gold and silver, you may
> recite the sutras, practice meditation, and even lead
> your daily lives in strict accordance with the pre-
> cepts, but if you carry on these activities without
> having the eye of *kenshō*, everyone of you belongs
> to the tribe of evil spirits.
> On the other hand, if you carry on your activities
> with the eye of *kenshō*, though you pass your days
> living in a solitary hut in the wilderness, wear a tat-
> tered robe, and eat only boiled roots, you are the
> man who meets me face to face every day and re-
> quites my kindness.[2]

This eye of *kenshō* is the Zen attitude of mind, resulting
largely from *satori*, by which one leads one's life seeing
into the nature of things. It might be called a quasi-
mystical vision of reality *as it is*, though the author of
the above might not approve of this definition, for he
declares: "If you ask me the question 'What is *kenshō*,'
what is this 'seeing into one's own real nature'? I am
afraid I can give you no other answer than to say:
'*Kenshō* is just *kenshō*, nothing more.'"[3]

Be that as it may, everything in Zen is oriented toward enlightenment and toward the preservation of its
spirit once found. Only the enlightened man can become
a master and a recognized director of others; only the
enlightened person can speak with real authority. And
in this sense Zen can be called completely mystical:
without enlightenment the whole structure falls to the
ground.

Christianity, on the other hand, though it contains a
strong current of mysticism, it not essentially mystical.
If one wanted to push the parallel with Buddhism, of
course, it might be argued that Christianity, too, is
founded on the mystical (and Trinitarian) experience of
Christ, who reveals the Father to the world; and it

might also be maintained that the Christian life is a re-enactment of the life of Christ in a modern setting. But this parallel is not too exact. For the Christian life can be lived in full vigor without any enlightenment like *satori;* no one need feel in the depth of his spirit the psychological shock of enlightenment or even the tranquillity of the prayer of quiet; those who speak with authority make no claim to mystical enlightenment. The true Christian enlightenment comes after death, and even the most profound experience in this world is no more than a pale shadow of the future reality. For this reason, in the long process which precedes the canonization of a Christian saint, the Church never asks about the profundity of his enlightenment or the depths of his mysticism, but only about his practice of heroic charity; traditionally, mysticism is valued only as a means to something more important—namely, the charity which is the center of the gospel message. When this charity expresses itself in mystical experience (that is, when the love of God becomes so violent that it drives the soul down into its very center in mystical darkness and existential abandonment of thought), then it is inestimably precious. But if a mystical mode of thought is divorced from charity or induced by means other than charity, then, however great its cultural and philosophical value, it cannot be called a central feature of the Christian life. In other words, mysticism as such has not been extolled by Christianity: it is always a way to, or an expression of, charity.

Granted this, however, everyone must recognize that deep contemplative prayer is indeed a way (and perhaps the best way) to Christian charity; it has always held an honored place in the Christian life, and its importance in modern times is enhanced because it brings Christianity into contact with non-Christian religions. Indeed, without mysticism, dialogue with many of these religions may well be impossible.

Let us now, then, ask about the meaning of this much-controverted word.

II

In some ways the word "mysticism" is unfortunate. It is too much surrounded with an aura of the occult, stemming from its etymological origin, as though it spoke of something a little estoteric. The same is true of its Japanese equivalent, *shimpi*. This also suggests abnormal psychic experiences; it recalls Aldous Huxley and the addicts of lysergic acid diethylamide (LSD). Hence it is not surprising that so many Zen masters reject it, denying that their exercise is in any way mystical.

"Contemplation" is a much better word. Its Latin equivalent was the translation of the Greek *theōria*, which for Plato and Aristotle was the apex of the philosophical life, a supreme and magnificent act in which one intuitively grasped the truth in an instantaneous flash accompanied by great joy. Aristotle (usually so dry) speaks enthusiastically about these moments in which man's life is already like that of God, moments in which he tastes that real happiness for which he exists. But alas, says the realistic Stagirite, man cannot long maintain these ecstatic moments (Eliot's "human kind cannot bear very much reality"), and so he must fall back to his merely human life, enlightened only by that "imperfect happiness" which stems from the good life.[4]

Such contemplation as this is the fruit of dialectical and syllogistic thinking; it is the climax of an intense effort of thought. But medieval Europe knew also a contemplation of a different kind; it knew the passive, dark, negative mysticism with its strong Neoplatonic flavor which had been gradually Christianized by Dionysius, Augustine, the Rhineland mystics, the author of *The Cloud of Unknowing*, and the rest. This was a species of what I have called vertical thinking, a process in which the mind goes silently down into its own center, revealing cavernous depths ordinarily latent and untouched by the flow of images and concepts that pass across the surface of the mind. It is that mysticism in which one descends to the "still point" or to the ground of the soul, thus finding a type of knowledge that is supraconceptual and therefore ineffable, a species of superthinking whereby one grasps the unity of all things —a unity which becomes increasingly apparent as one's knowledge becomes more and more existentially voided of concepts, images, quiddities, and essences to remain utterly silent and receptive. And the silent devotion to this kind of thinking produces a certain liberation or detachment which is the fruit of a deep interiority. This is the apophatic mysticism of darkness which is complemented by the cataphatic mysticism of light found in Bernard of Clairvaux and the others less attracted by the silent passivity of the void.

From this it can be seen that already in medieval Europe, before explicit knowledge of Oriental religions came on the scene, the many streams and varieties of mysticism and contemplation created a complex problem. This was further complicated by the difficulty of finding a common definition for that contemplation which was totally Christocentric (and all genuine Christian contemplation is just that) and for that Hellenic and Neoplatonic brand of contemplation which knew nothing of Christ.

Aquinas, however, seems to have solved this problem with serene transcendentalism, and without any trace of that narrow intolerance which we associate with that period simplistically and incorrectly referred to as the Dark Ages. Far from denying that the "pagans" are contemplatives, he gives the broadest possible definition of contemplation, which puts everyone, Christian and non-Christian, into one category. For him, contemplation is "a simple intuition of the truth" (*simplex intuitus veritatis*).[5] He who attains truth and rests in it is contemplative.

Yet Aquinas does not say that all forms of contemplation are the same. He was not given to such oversimplification. The distinct feature of Christian contemplation, separating it from anything in the Hellenic world, was

that the truth intuited is the fruit of faith and charity.
An intense love welling up within the heart of him
who believes enlightens the intelligence, which is now
flooded with a new knowledge, no longer stemming from
discursive reasoning. This is the truest wisdom, which
only love can engender. Superior to logical thinking, it
is a deepening of the gift of wisdom common to all who
love God; and this knowledge is called by St. Thomas
"connatural," since it arises from consciousness of one's
union with God in love. Its nature is beautifully expressed by the author of *The Cloud of Unknowing* in a
traditional metaphor:

> As when the candel burneth, thou mayest see the
> candel itself by the light thereof, and other things
> also; right so when thy soul burneth in the love of
> God, that is when thou feelest continuously thine
> heart desire after the love of God, then by the light
> of his grace which he sendeth in thy reason, thou
> mayest both see thine unworthiness and his great
> goodness. And therefore . . . profer thy candel to
> the fire.[6]

So here in the Middle Ages we find a generic definition
of a contemplation including everyone, Greek or Christian, who attains to the truth, side by side with a specific
Christian contemplation grounded on faith in, and love
for, Christ.

III

Coming now to modern times, one wonders if the intro-
duction of Oriental mysticism to the West (and especially Zen, which interests us here) need really modify
this theological doctrine so much; perhaps the whole
problem can still be studied within the Thomistic framework. At first sight, of course, the silent, cross-legged
sitting of Zen might seem utterly removed from anything known to Aquinas, but a second glance shows that
it bears resemblances even to the *theōria* of Aristotle. In
both cases long hours are devoted to preparatory

thought and intense concentration, which culminates in a momentary flash of tremendous light. Both demand ascetical preparation and the practice of virtue. In both cases enlightenment is taken as the end and aim of man's life in which he finds his truest happiness. In both cases there is a certain reticence about the exact content and nature of the experience itself (it is surprising how Aristotle, usually so devastatingly analytical, becomes mystically reserved on this point). Again, in both cases it can be said that there is a sense of union or "oneness" with all things; and here again Aristotle, contrary to everything he writes elsewhere, comes so near to a species of pantheism that Averroist interpreters claimed that he was propounding a world soul, a *nous* that was the same in all men.[7] Finally, in both cases the search for enlightenment is not just an escapist flight from the world; just as the Bodhisattva vows to save all sentient beings, so the Greek philosopher comes back to the world to work for social and political reform.

Where Zen and Aristotle part company is in the former's silence, passivity, emptying of the mind, suppression of thought and imagery—all which is foreign to the way of thinking of the active, peripatetic Greek. Yet a somewhat similar state is found in the Neoplatonic stream of apophatic mysticism to which I have already referred. So striking is the similarity between this way of thinking and certain branches of Oriental mysticism that scholars of no small name hold that they had a common origin in a certain type of shamanism in India, the Eastern version of which was to influence Yoga, Mahayana Buddhism, and (after its meeting with Taoism) Zen, while the Western version branched out into Gnosticism and Neoplatonism, which in turn greatly influenced the negative theology of Eastern Christianity.[8] Be that as it may (for much of this remains hypothetical, and similarities may be the result of "anthropism," arising from a common human nature), many elements of Zen meditation were known to medieval Europe; and it seems to me that the same Thomistic definition which

includes Aristotelian *theōria* and Christian mysticism can
also be applied to the Zen *satori* and to any other
religious or philosophical experience which genuinely
grasps the truth: all can be put in one category as
contemplatio, a simple intuition of the truth.

IV

If, then, the teaching of Aquinas had been preserved
and developed, there might have been less theological
confusion in defining mysticism today. As it was, post-
Reformation Catholic theology pursued a slightly different line of thought, based upon its own conception
of grace; and when, at the beginning of this century,
Christianity came face to face with non-Christian mysticism, the theologians' handling of the problem was less
felicitous than that of their angelic forerunner when he
confronted the Greeks. It was clear to everyone that the
non-Christian experiences ought to be called mysticism
in some sense of the word; but what was the nature of
this mysticism? What was its relationship to Christianity?
Was it the work of grace? These were the crucial questions. While the theologians of the day must have been
willing, at least theoretically, to admit that God's grace
was at work outside the visible Church, they were reluctant to admit that non-Christian mysticism might be
the result of grace—which for them was something of a
superstructure added to the Christian at baptism and
working with special vigor in the mystic. Christian
mysticism was the expression of a special grace which
the non-Christian could rarely have (and if he did have
it, he was already a Christian and the problem was
solved); so they coined the term "natural mysticism" for
the non-Christian experience as opposed to the "supernatural mysticism" of the Christian: Christian mysticism
was performed with the help of grace, non-Christian
mysticism by unaided nature alone. In this way the
presence or absence of grace was the dividing line that

separated the Christian mystic from his non-Christian counterpart.

Yet this way of thinking and speaking is unsatisfactory. For one thing, it necessarily irritates the non-Christian, who feels that some crumbs of "nature" are thrown to him while the Christian basks in the complacency of "supernature." Furthermore, non-Christians have great difficulty in understanding the theological meaning of "supernatural" and sometimes take it (erroneously, of course) that Christians are claiming a phenomenological superiority for their mysticism, as though it were something much more psychologically profound than what is found in other religions. But apart from this, there is the fact that orthodox theology recognizes no "natural" state, everyone being either in grace or in sin. The theologians, of course, in their effort to avoid ascribing grace to the non-Christian, were trying to describe a hypothetical state of man left to himself; but since such a state does not exist, the whole solution as applied to the concrete, existential situation of the non-Christian mystic was not satisfactory.

In the post-conciliar Church, however, reluctance to admit that non-Christians have grace and are helped by God has given place to an attitude which sees the working of the Holy Spirit in all religions. It is possible now to say with Rahner that "theology has been led astray for too long by the tacit assumption that grace would be no longer grace if God became too free with it." [9] That non-Christians may have grace no one will now deny; that in consequence their mysticism may in some sense be supernatural can be maintained. Nor is this to go to the other extreme, asserting that everyone is in grace and that all mysticism is supernatural; rather is it to say that in a given case we simply do not know and have no means of finding out with certainty, since grace is so intimately intertwined with nature that it does not fall within the scope of observation and clinical psychology; but in doubt it is not unreasonable to presume with

Rahner that the non-Christian is moved by grace, that he is an anonymous Christian. In distinguishing between Christian and non-Christian mysticism, therefore, it seems to me much better to abandon the whole nature-*versus*-supernature approach and return to the Thomistic norm, which is an empirical one and acceptable to non-Christians: namely, mysticism which arises from, and culminates in, love of God in Christ is Christian; that which does not (but yet remains a simple intuition of the truth) is non-Christian. Nor does the Christian claim that his experiences are deeper, more soul-stirring, more phenomenologically extraordinary than those of his non-Christian brother. As for the question where nature ends and supernature begins—this need not even be asked and cannot be answered, for supernature is normally so bound up with nature that its working in a given instance cannot be detected.

V

If, however, nineteenth-century theologians found it difficult to define Oriental mysticism, they found no less difficulty in disentangling "nature" and "supernatural" elements in their own Christian mysticism; and once again the whole difficulty arose from the conception of grace. A theory was worked out that by one's own efforts one could "acquire" certain degrees of prayer (these were classified as "discursive prayer," "affective prayer," and "the prayer of simplicity"), but beyond this no one could go with his own efforts but must wait for the purely gratuitous gift of "infused contemplation," which God gave to some and not to others according to His free election. Thus René de Maumigny, in his well-known book on mental prayer, *Pratique de l'oraison mentale*, clearly draws the dividing line between "ordinary" and "extraordinary" prayer at the point where silence predominates in the interior life. In general, spiritual writers agreed that silence, passive receptivity, emptiness, and darkness were not to be spoken of much,

for they were "pure gifts," belonging to the category of
"prayer which cannot be taught" as opposed to the
active "prayer which can be taught." Mystical prayer
was a special grace, a special superstructure imposed
upon the prayer life of the ordinary Christian by God,
who gave it to some and not to others.

And yet perhaps all this needs some rethinking—for
several reasons. First of all, according to orthodox theology, no prayer can be acquired or taught. Taking
literally the words of Christ "Without me you can do
nothing," the Church has defined that even to call on
God demands a grace from Him. What these theologians
meant, of course (for they knew this doctrine well
enough), was that infused contemplation in passive receptivity could not be reached without a "special grace"
—though it is not at all easy to determine the nature
of this special grace, nor is there clear evidence for its
existence in the scriptures and in the official tradition
of the Church. Some modern theologians (notably
Reginald Garrigou-Lagrange) have gone to great pains
to show that infused contemplation is not quite so
"special" and that the notion of a special mystical path
mysteriously opened before "chosen" souls is not completely in keeping with the Christian tradition as it existed up to and including Aquinas, for whom there was
only one way, that of an ever-growing charity leading
to the truest wisdom—as I have already pointed out.
This was the path of every Christian.

It is difficult, then, to see the theological foundation
for a clear-cut distinction between prayer which can be
taught and that which cannot. At any rate, it is difficult
to see why anyone should point to a certain stage in
prayer, saying: "Here starts the special grace: simple
prayer is the border line, silence marks the advance into
extraordinary prayer." If the old theologians meant that
silence and wordless concentration in the absence of
thoughts and images cannot be attained by ordinary
human endeavor, then they were wrong, as is clearly
proved by Oriental mysticisms, which *as far as concen-*

tration is concerned seem to be little different from the Christian counterpart. Friedrich Heiler tells us:

> Although the descriptions of the stages of prayer, their number and their characteristics, vary, yet there is no essential difference between the neo-Platonic, Sûfi, Hindu, and Christian mystics; their basic psychological character is identical even with the stages of absorption in the Yoga and in Buddhism, though in the latter every notion of prayer, that is, communion with God, is excluded.[10]

It may be that the nineteenth-century notion of a special grace from on high was given some impetus from the fact (attested by many mystics) that infused contemplation is often beyond the control of the person who enjoys it: it comes a little mysteriously at unexpected times and places, while it may be absent in times of formal prayer. This may have made people think that God was intervening in some extraordinary way that was psychologically inexplicable. But with the advance in depth psychology, we know that the unconscious from which this concentration arises can play all sorts of unpredictable tricks, surging into consciousness when one least expects it; the exact moment when the horizon of consciousness will be expanded can never be accurately foretold, and so (once again) this very unexpectedness does not give reason for drawing a clear line of demarcation: here the action of man ends and God takes over.

The statement of Heiler I have quoted refers to stages of absorption—in which line it seems difficult, perhaps impossible, to distinguish Christian mysticism from others. If, then, we wish to set Christian mysticism apart, we can only do so by a theological definition. And I have tried to say that the best definition is not that Christian mysticism is performed with grace and is supernatural, whereas the other is natural (for of this we can have no surety), but that Christian contemplation is found in that wisdom which arises from a deep love of God in Christ, and that it reaches its climax in an experience of unity and separation that mirrors the Blessed Trinity. This is the Thomistic definition, which, I believe, non-Christians will gladly recognize.

This theological definition alone, however, is not sufficient for the spiritual guide whose chief interest is in giving direction to the mystic. For this reason it must be supplemented by a phenomenological description.

VI

To understand the phenomenological aspect of mysticism, it is necessary to go back to the Reformation with its stress on the inner light and on religious experience as a norm of action. This had been something of a break with a medieval tradition characterized by objectivity and much less preoccupied with subjective reactions and feelings. And in the field of mysticism the medieval distrust of subjectivism was especially evident. In the course of the search for God (immanent and transcendent), certain psychic phenomena such as ecstasy or what the moderns call "increased perception" might arise, but the orthodox medieval directors, wary of such phenomena, constantly put the contemplative on his guard against them with the warning that what one feels or experiences is not God Himself in His essence— for God is above anything one can feel or experience in this life. Furthermore, traditional spirituality always put obedience to the director (who stood for the Church) above trust in one's private interior motions. Later, Teresa of Avila is to show extraordinary distrust of her own subjective feelings, which she always puts second to her director's counsel.

With the Reformation, however, begins the strong subjectivism, the rejection of priests and dogma in favor of the inner light and attention to the voice of God, which (in spite of its many excellent aspects) reaches an unfortunate climax in a tendency to reject everything except the inner light: it does not really matter if Christ existed or not, if the scriptures are historical or not, if the

Church is apostolic or not—the only thing that matters
is my inner experience, my meeting with Christ in
prayer. In short, religious experience occupies the center
of the picture.

Now, of all religious experience, the most fascinat-
ingly interesting is that of the mystic. And so a good
deal of popular Christianity since the turn of the century
has occupied itself with the psychological states of this
enigmatic figure—with his feelings, his visions, his darkness, his anxiety, his dark nights, his revelations, his
ecstasies, and so on. And once again the same pattern
appears: it does not matter whether or not these feelings
correspond to anything real; it does not matter whether
or not the God of the mystics really exists; what matters
is the religious experience, the increased perception, the
ecstasy. Gone is the time when these phenomena were
considered dangerous distractions; now they are an end
in themselves. The Rhineland mystics, St. John of the
Cross, and the author of *The Cloud of Unknowing* had
intransigently forbidden any search for psychic anomalies (which, however, they recognized might sometimes accompany a true love of God), and the "nothing,
nothing, nothing" of the Spanish mystic as well as the
"cloud of forgetting" of the anonymous Englishman precisely meant that one should be completely detached
from ecstasies, consolations, clairvoyance, visions, or any
of these phenomena which fall under the modern terminology of "increased perception." St. John of the Cross
goes so far as to say that "all visions, revelations, and
feelings *coming from heaven,* and any thoughts that may
proceed from these, are of less worth than the least act
of humility." [11] He was only concerned with the love of
God and the fulfillment of the first commandment; the
bringing into play of ordinarily latent mystical faculties
was a by-product of little importance. But now the
tables are turned, and the subjective feelings that were
previously a by-product are the goal.

But if religious experience is so important, it might
be a good idea to stimulate it, and thus arises the use of

drugs as a way to mysticism. The best-known experimenter in this line is, of course, Aldous Huxley, whose little book *The Doors of Perception* told of the inner world of mystical space that the author had discovered under the influence of mescalin. A religious adventurer Huxley may have been, but no one can deny his brilliance as a writer. Anguished man, he insists, feels an irresistible need to escape, to transcend self, to get away from the drab world; and of all the possible ways of achieving this transcendence, mescalin, which induces mystical experience, is the least innocuous and most successful. ("All I am suggesting is that the mescalin experience is what Catholic theologians call 'a gratuitous gift,' not necessary to salvation but potentially helpful and to be accepted thankfully if made available.") The sometimes tragic subsequent history of mescalin need not occupy us here. Some years ago, while visiting a Zen monastery far out in the countryside at the foot of Mount Fuji, I was astonished to hear the good Rōshi refer to an article about "instant Zen" in *Time*, where it was indicated that LSD might be a short-cut to *satori*. The monk smiled good-humoredly. He neither affirmed nor denied. But his smile bespoke what was in his heart.

VII

Yet the growing interest in states of consciousness which has characterized the last fifty or sixty years has led to the appearance of significant and useful phenomenological studies which might well have done a great service to Christian spiritual direction, if only the theologians and psychologists had succeeded in getting together a little earlier in a joint effort to solve their problems. Jung, indeed, frequently expressed his desire to collaborate with theologians, and he wrote a preface to a theological work.[12] But this was exceptional. Pre-conciliar mystical theology was not too eager to cooperate, and only in comparatively recent times has a real mutual understanding begun to develop.

At the beginning of the century, William James gave a descriptive definition of mysticism intended to cover a wide variety of experiences. Writing before the rise of Suzuki, he seems to have been unfamiliar with Zen— which, however, fits neatly into his categories, showing how remarkably worldwide this mystical pattern is. As chief characteristics of mysticism he singles out first of all *ineffability*: the mystics state that their condition cannot be expressed or communicated to others. He puts it well:

> One must have musical ears to know the value of a symphony; one must have been in love oneself to understand a lover's state of mind. Lacking the heart or ear, we cannot interpret the musician or the lover justly, and are even likely to consider him weak-minded or absurd. The mystic finds that most of us accord to his experiences an equally incompetent treatment.[13]

The second characteristic according to James is a certain *noetic* quality. In mystical states one attains to true knowledge: "They are states of insight into depths of truth unplumbed by the discursive intellect. They are illuminations, revelations, full of significance and importance, all inarticulate though they remain. . . ."[14] This again is true both of genuine Christian mysticism and of Zen. In neither case does one sit in utter vacuity; rather, there is an attainment of really supraconceptual knowledge (which explains why everything is nothing and vacuity is plenitude). The Cartesian trend in Western thought has tended to assume that knowledge can be found only in clear and distinct ideas; but mystical knowledge, dark and obscure, has nothing to do with concepts. That is why it is ineffable; but it is true knowledge.

James ends his definition with these two characteristics; but he adds two other qualities usually found. The first is *transience*. This, I believe, is true of the highest states of mysticism (though even these may be prolonged for days at the summit of the mystical life). But the deep sense of the presence of God and the *samadhi* of Zen, ineffable and noetic though they be, are not always transient but continue almost unbrokenly in the lives of some persons.

The second quality is *passivity:* "when the characteristic sort of consciousness once has set in, the mystic feels as if his own will were in abeyance, and indeed sometimes as if he were grasped and held by a superior power." This is certainly true of many forms of mysticism, including Christian. It probably would not be accepted by some Zen masters who determinedly reject all suggestions of being grasped by "a superior power"; but others, such as Dōgen, assert that in the greatest moments of enlightenment they were grasped by something greater than themselves.

It seems to me, then, that James's description, stressing the ineffability and noetic quality, and suggesting that transience and passivity are often present, is a good phenomenological definition.

VIII

Now let us attempt to find a comprehensive definition. The complexities of the matter under discussion can only be dealt with by approaching the problem from three angles: philosophical, theological, and phenomenological.

First of all, philosophical. I have expressed my opinion that the best philosophical definition is the Thomistic "simple intuition of the truth." This covers Christian mysticism, Hellenic and Neoplatonic contemplation, and Zen. All these can, I think, be truly said to culminate in an intuitive grasp of the truth which becomes increasingly "simple" in proportion as duality (particularly subject—object duality) is lost in an experience of unity. But can this definition cover experiments like Huxley's? Here I would say no—if the subject, far from seeking truth, is trying to escape from it. And Aldous Huxley avowedly is doing just this.

Then the theological aspect. I have referred to the
Thomistic contention that faith in, and love for, God in
Christ enlightens the mind with high wisdom. In other
words, what is special to Christian mysticism, both in its
initial and final stages, is precisely this sapiential and
unitive love. Such a way of speaking is, I believe,
eminently suitable, and the Zen Rōshi would readily
agree that their exercise does not fit into this category.

As for the drugs, if they do not induce mysticism in
the philosophical sense, a fortiori they have nothing to
do with theology.

Thirdly, there is the phenomenological aspect. Here
the description of William James remains, I believe, sub-
stantially accurate and acceptable. Perhaps it is most
significant in pointing out that mysticism plunges downward, opening up a new and deep level of the psyche
untouched by discursive thinking and reasoning. And
again, while admitting that it covers both the Zen and
the Christian experience, we might ask if a similar psychological condition is induced by the mescalin experiment of Huxley.

It seems true, indeed, that certain drugs can touch
the same level of psychic life as does mysticism, actuat-
ing the same faculties and enabling one to see into the
essence of things in a way similar to Zen. Indeed, James
himself indicates that "the drunken consciousness is one
bit of the mystic consciousness." Intoxicants, anesthetics,
and alchohol, he feels, have a "mystical" effect: "The
sway of alcohol over mankind is unquestionably due to
its power to stimulate the mystical faculties of human
nature, usually crushed to earth by the cold facts and
dry criticisms of the sober hour." [15] All this has led some
scholars to the conclusion that drugs like mescalin may
perhaps induce a genuine mystical experience in the
phenomenological sense. Even Professor Stace, a much-
esteemed writer on mysticism, can assert that

> those who have achieved mystical states as a result
> of long and arduous spiritual exercises, fasting and
> prayer, or great moral efforts, possibly spread over

many years, are inclined to deny that a drug can induce a "genuine" mystical experience, or at least to
look askance at such practices and such a claim. Our
principle says that *if* the phenomenological descriptions of the two experiences are indistinguishable, so
far as can be ascertained, then it cannot be denied
that if one is a genuine mystical experience the other
is also. This will follow notwithstanding the lowly
antecedents of one of them, and in spite of the understandable annoyance of an ascetic, a saint, or a
spiritual hero, who is told that his careless and worldly
neighbour, who never did anything to deserve it, has
attained to mystical consciousness by swallowing a
pill.[16]

And yet I would be reluctant to call such experiences
mystical, even in the phenomenological sense. The reason is that the true mystical descent to the core of one's
being is always accompanied by progress in mortal virtue
and in psychic maturity, and it effects a reform or a conversion or whatever it may be. In Christian mysticism it
has always been the moral norm, formulated in the so-
called "Rules for the Discernment of Spirits," that de-
termines the validity of mystical experiences. But in the
use of drugs no such moral change is evident: Aldous
Huxley himself made no claim to have grown in virtue
after swallowing the mescalin. There is as yet no evidence for the existence of a drug that effects the detachment and the serenity resulting from silent meditation.
And all this indicates a profound difference between the
experiences. Stace, preoccupied with phenomenology
alone, seems to assume that his ascetic, saint, and
spiritual hero were looking for some delectable experience. But they were not. They were looking for God
and cared little about what they experienced. Besides,
even phenomenologically one cannot judge only by what
a person experiences at the moment; one must also take
into account the transformation and conversion (or lack
of it) which follows.

Indeed, in this whole context the term "false mysticism" (little in vogue today) may not be inept. For

Huxley's experimentation is not so new as might at first sight appear. Even the medievals knew that the by-products or side-effects of mysticism could be produced by means other than prayer to God; and so they used the term "false mysticism" with all its grotesque overtones. They knew well enough that the pure spiritual joy accompanying the "intensified perception" (to use again the modern term) of mystical experience was something so delectable that any reasonable man would sacrifice the grossest pleasures of sense to obtain it; they knew that even the genuine mystics may easily fall into the trap of mistaking the by-product for the reality; they knew well the dangers of seeking the pleasures of mysticism without seeking God. And so they stressed the danger of undue emphasis on phenomenological aspects as norms of genuineness. Nor was Huxley ignorant of all this; for some of the most lurid passages in his novels depict the absurdities and obscenities of false mysticism, or they describe the unscrupulous, ambitious politician who in the name of mysticism and with a reputation for sanctity wants to influence the masses and speak with the voice of God. And apart from these enormities, he knew of those who imagine that they are in the night of sense when they are half-asleep or who imagine that they are undergoing diabolic assaults when they are disturbed and ill. Yet, if we simply define mysticism as the actuation of a certain consciousness ordinarily dormant, all this is brought into one category without distinction.[17]

In conclusion, then, it can be said that a scientific consideration of the question demands this threefold approach, and that if one is lacking the whole thing may become lopsided. The philosophical definition enables adherents of various religions to find common ground for dialogue. The theological definition points to the specific difference between mysticisms of the different religions, saving us from relativism and from the oversimplification that "all are the same." The phenomenological definition, besides giving the raw material for the other two, provides valuable practical knowledge which is of the utmost necessity for skilled spiritual direction. Zen and Christian mysticism can be classed together philosophically and phenomenologically—but not theologically. Nor does this mean that phenomenologically they are exactly the same (for experiences that differ theologically could not be identical phenomenologically); but that they are sufficiently similar to be put in the same generic classification. Thus is paved the way for a dialogue based, not upon common dogmas, but upon common religious experience.

Finally, our consideration of comparative mysticism in conjunction with modern psychology makes it clear that Christian mystical theology needs a thorough updating. We have had too many divisions and subdivisions—into acquired and infused, ordinary and extraordinary, prayer of simplicity, of simple regard, of varying degrees of union, and so on; and the theologians (or perhaps the spiritual directors who follow them) have been too quick to step in and say: "The direct action of God starts here."

The post-conciliar era has seen a wonderful *aggiornamento* in liturgy, scriptural studies, and in religious life; but the *aggiornamento* in mystical theology remains to be done. We can be grateful to Oriental mysticism and depth psychology for the light they will bring in this regard.

NOTES

1. Daisetsu T. Suzuki, *Essays in Zen Buddhism*, First Series (London, 1958), p. 230.
2. Miura and Sasaki, *Zen Kôan*, p. 38.
3. *Ibid.*, p. 37.
4. Cf. *Nicomachean Ethics*, Bk. 10.
5. *Summa theol.* 2a 2ae, q. 180, a. 3, ad 1m.
6. *A Tretyse of the Stodye of Wysdome.*
7. It was against this interpretation, by Siger of Brabant, that Thomas wrote *De Unitate intellectus.*
8. Cf. Etienne Cornélis, "Christian Spirituality and Non-Christian Spiritualities," *Concilium*, 9 (1965), pp. 81–

90, where the author quotes Dodd and Eliade as holding this theory. The extent of the Indian influence on Neoplatonism remains uncertain. We know, however, that in the early Christian era Alexandria was a crossroad between East and West and that there was trade between its port and the ports of India. It is just possible that there was a Buddhist colony in this great city. Here there was a library containing the most famous books of Greece, Israel, Persia, and India; Plotinus went to the East with the Emperor Gordian and may even have gone as far as India.

9. Rahner, *Nature and Grace*, p. 133.
10. Friedrich Heiler, *Prayer: A Study in the History and Psychology of Religion*, trans. Samuel McComb (New York, 1958), p. 194.
11. John of the Cross, *The Ascent of Mount Carmel*, Bk. III, ch. IX, 4.
12. See Jung's Foreword to Victor White, *God and the Unconscious* (Chicago, 1953).
13. James, *Varieties of Religious Experience*, p. 367.
14. *Ibid.*
15. *Ibid.*, p. 373.
16. W. T. Stace, *Mysticism and Philosophy* (London, 1961), pp. 29–30.
17. Though I have denied that drugs can induce mystical experience, it is not my intention to state categorically that experimentation with them is useless and pernicious or that it is necessarily linked with escapism. In fact, the increased perception which they effect may perhaps cure neurosis by uncovering diseased parts of the mind and tapping the unconscious. Furthermore, this experimentation opens up immense possibilities of investigating a sector of the mind not linked to time and space.

9

INCARNATION

I

In any dialogue between Christianity and other religions, the crux is obviously the Incarnation; the problem is particularly acute in the field of comparative mysticism. On other points there can be agreement, harmony, similarity of approach. The silence, the void, the passive receptivity, the existential detachment, the descent to the core of one's being or to the still point—everything included in what I have called "vertical meditation" can be found in many cultures and religions, so that a mystical dialogue is not out of question. But then in Christianity there appears the man Christ; and dialogue falls to pieces. For what role can a man, a real man of flesh and blood, play in this void of silence? And yet Christianity *is* Christ; it proclaims Him as the way, the Truth, and the Life. Prayer which bypassed Christ would be a travesty of Christianity. Claiming that Christ is the Eternal Word of God made flesh, Christianity is obliged to give Him a place which Buddhism could not yield to the Buddha or Islam to Mohammed. Zen contains nothing even vaguely resembling dialogue with Christ and meditation on His words.

II

This problem is not new. Christ the man was a scandal from the beginning; and a religion of the Word made flesh soon found itself in conflict with religions of pure spirit. Gnosticism, Neoplatonism, Manichaeism, and the rest could scarcely be expected to countenance a God of flesh and blood nailed to a cross, giving His body to His disciples, speaking through men, and granting salvation with the instrumentality of water. Something so utterly incarnational and fleshly inevitably clashed with spiritual gnosticism in a conflict which, perhaps, has not been fully resolved to this very day. And at the center of this conflict was the tremendous question: can an incarnational religion like Christianity produce a genuine mysticism?

A posteriori, of course, it could be convincingly argued that Christianity can nourish a powerful mystical life. Augustine, Gregory, Bernard, and Teresa are there to prove it. But the objection has been raised that even these giants felt an intolerable tension between their Catholicism and their mysticism. This thesis has been brilliantly expounded by Aldous Huxley who maintains that the genuine apophatic mysticism, which came from India to Neoplatonism and was transmitted to the Christian tradition through the "pious fraud" of Dionysius, is quite incompatible with an orthodox and Biblical Christianity inextricably bound to the man called Jesus Christ. Catholicism, he feels (and especially that brand taught by the Jesuits), has done its utmost to destroy genuine mysticism by urging a kind of prayer centered on meditation on the person of Christ, on His virtues, His qualities, His words—a meditative exercise which is incompatible with the supraconceptual silence of mystical prayer. Huxley says:

> Contemplation of persons and their qualities entails a great deal of analytic thinking and an incessant use of the imagination. But analytic thinking and imagination are precisely the things which prevent the soul from attaining enlightenment. On this point all the great mystical writers, Christian and oriental, are unanimous and emphatic. Consequently, the would-be mystic who chooses as the object of his love and contemplation, not the Godhead, but a person and personal qualities, thereby erects insur-

mountable barriers between himself and the higher
states of union.[1]

In this way, the orthodox Catholic mystics who tried
to unite the silent darkness of pure spirit with meditation about the man Christ have found themselves enmeshed in a terrible struggle between their Catholicism
and their mysticism, and have ended up by rejecting
one or the other.

Huxley alone might not be a formidable adversary.
But he quotes one of the leading Catholic spiritual
writers of the century. Abbot John Chapman writes of
the difficulty of reconciling (not merely uniting) mysticism with Christianity and refers to Abbot Marmion
who said that St. John of the Cross is like a sponge full
of Christianity—you can squeeze it all out and the full
mystical theory remains. Consequently, says Marmion,
for fifteen years or so he hated St. John of the Cross and
called him a Buddhist, but loved St. Teresa and read
her again and again. After all, she was first a Christian
and only secondarily a mystic.

Now, to say a word first about the Abbot Marmion's
sponge. Though his point is valid, I do not see that it
makes John of the Cross any less Christian than Teresa.
After all, a sponge can contain water or milk or tea; and
the same mystical sponge can contain Christianity, Hin-
duism, or Buddhism. The all-important thing is the
content. The human sponge is the same everywhere,
and this accounts for the striking similarities in all religious experience. Christian mysticism reaches its peak-
point when the psychic life is filled to overflowing with
faith and love: Buddhist mysticism reaches its peak-
point in another way.

This, however, does not solve Huxley's problem that
"analytic thinking and imagination are precisely the
things that prevent the soul from attaining enlightenment." This is true: the highest prayer is wordless and
has nothing to do with discursive reasoning. But it
seems to me that Huxley is misled, because he takes the
discursive meditation taught in the *Spiritual Exercises*

of St. Ignatius as the whole of Christian prayer. And
of course it is not. The so-called Ignatian prayer (and
this is something of a misnomer because Ignatius did
not pray this way) is only one stage, and an initial
stage, in a spiritual ascent spiralling up to a realm in
which Christ is present—but without words, images,
and thoughts. In that mysticism of which John of the
Cross is the chief exponent, Christ is present *but not as
an object of meditation*: He is present within. I have already said that the highest Christian mysticism is Trinitarian: it is an identification with Christ who offers
Himself to the Father in the Holy Spirit. The mystics
speak of Christ as continuing His incarnation within
them, taking over their bodies to be His own. And to
vindicate this way of thinking they constantly appeal to
the Pauline "I live, now not I, but Christ liveth in me."
But their way of thinking calls for more explanation.

III

Perhaps we should first get clear what is entailed by
this word Incarnation. If it simply meant that God became man for thirty years or so and then went back to
heaven, the whole of Christianity would be centered on
these thirty historical years, on meditation on the person who lived in Nazareth, on looking back on a past
to which Christians were inextricably bound. Then, too,
prayer which abandoned "analytic thinking and imagination" might be regarded with suspicion as something
which rejected Christ the man. But does the Incarnation mean only this?

Catholic theology teaches that when the Word became flesh He united Himself through the humanity of
Christ with all men who believe: Christ Himself re-
peatedly says that He came to give life, to give it more
abundantly, to share with others the divine life that
was His by right. He was the vine from which the
branches of humanity took their life; He was the bread
that gives life to the world; He was the life in which all

could share. That is why the early fathers of the Church
(especially the Greek fathers) spoke of the divinization
of the human race through Christ, or said with Augustine that God became man in order that man might become God. For the same Augustine loves to say that

> Christ is not merely in the head and not in the body,
> but the whole Christ is in the head and in the body.
> And, therefore, he is what his members are; but his
> members are not necessarily what he is. Were his
> members not himself, he would not have said to Saul:
> "Why do you persecute me?" For Saul was persecut-
> ing on earth, not him, but his members, that is, the
> faithful. And yet he did not choose to say "my saints"
> or "my servants" or, more honorably still, "my breth-
> ren," but: "me," that is, "my members, of whom I
> am the head."

In short, by the Incarnation God linked Himself through
Christ with the human race: and He came to stay.

All this means that the true Christian life develops
to its fullest richness, not merely by looking at the historical Christ from the outside and imitating His virtues, not merely by Aldous Huxley's "analytic thinking
and imagination"; rather, it is a question of "becoming"
Christ—the Christian asks that the life of Christ may
well up within him, transforming him into "another
Christ." It is true that one way of "becoming Christ" is
to make use of the imaginative, discursive prayer that
played a central part in medieval piety, but this is not
the only way.

The Christian mystic has abandoned discursive
prayer about the person of Christ in favor of existential
silence, not in order to leave Christ, but in a sense to
become Christ. He believes that Christ is within and,
as Ruysbroeck well says, the coming of Christ to us is
from within outwards and we toward Him from without inwards. That is why John of the Cross centers so
much of his mysticism on the Pauline "I live, now not
I, but Christ liveth in me"; and other mystics will speak
of the life of Christ growing within them to such an

extent that they can say it is not I that sees: Christ sees
through my eyes; He listens through my ears; He
speaks through my lips; He blesses with my hands; He
loves through my heart. Christian mysticism is not a
looking at Christ and an imitation of Him, but a transformation into Christ. It is as though the Word who
became flesh as a Jew wants to relive His life in other
persons, in other times, in other cultures, in another
historical setting.

In order, however, that Christ may come to mystical
fullness within the Christian something must die; for
he that would save his life must lose it. If Christianity
demands a great death of everyone, much greater is
the death it asks from the mystic. For the "he that
would save his life must lose it" and the "I live, now
not I, but Christ liveth in me" have always had a special interpreation from the mystics.[2] All these phrases
about dying to self and losing self and so on that have
found such a central place in Christian ascetical literature have taken on a special meaning in the hands of
the mystics: I have already quoted how literally and
drastically the death to self is taken by the author of
The Cloud who speaks of the destruction of the self in
remarkable words. It is precisely in this death-to-self
way of speaking that Christian mysticism comes nearest
to the terminology of Buddhism, and it is precisely because of the nearness of that terminology that one must
make the necessary distinctions to see the difference
between the two. At all events, as we have already
seen, it is while analyzing the loss of the ego in the Zen
experience that Jung refers to St. Paul's loss of the ego
in his "I live, now not I, but Christ liveth in me": he
says that "it is as if the subject-character of the ego had
been overrun, or taken over, by another subject which
appears in place of the ego." [3]

And so we can understand how the cloud of forgetting, the nothingness, the void, the destruction of self
—all play a great part in Christian mysticism, being
preparatory to the finding of a real self in Christ. All

the negation is a preparation for the divinization of
man. And also one can understand the growing passivity, which is no more than a preparation for another
activity: that of Christ. The author of *The Cloud* expresses all this with the Johannine text "Without me
you can do nothing"; and he insists that the whole activity of the contemplative is nothing else than the activity of Christ Himself. "In deeds that be contemplative, he [Christ] is with us principally stirring and
working, and we go only but suffering and consenting."
In this way the passivity of Christian mysticism is only
a means to allow the life of Christ to well up vigorously
within the Christian (sometimes to such an extent that
he seems to lose his own ego), who now becomes an
instrument for an activity which history shows to be
incredibly powerful.

IV

From this it will be clear that Christian mysticism remains Christocentric without being bound up with analytic thinking and with reflection on persons and their
qualities: its passivity is an allowing of the life of
Christ to rise up within the heart and divinize the
whole personality. It is not even necessary to reflect
discursively in prayer upon the great dogmas of the
Trinity, the Redemption, and so on; for the mystic,
rather than looking at these truths like a spectator gaz-
ing from the outside, lives them in his very person: the
mystic, as we have seen, must be "naked of self to be
clothed in Christ" and offer himself to the Father for
the salvation of the human race as did Christ on the
Cross. In other words he has become another Christ,
re-enacting in his own life the work of redemption:
Christ living within him offers Himself once again to
the Father for the redemption of the world. And this is
the mystic interpretation of the thought of Paul who
gave up his own mind to put on the mind that was in
Christ Jesus, who with Christ was nailed to the cross,

who passed through the tomb with Christ, who rose
from the dead with Christ—"I live, now not I, but
Christ liveth in me." It is only by understanding this
identification with Christ with its consequently Trinitarian effects that one can understand the near-panthe-
ism of some of the Christian mystics. As Christ, the
Word of God, is of the same nature as the Father while
being distinct from Him in personality, so the mystic is,
by adoption, of one nature with God the Father while
remaining distinct in person. Here again we are at the
center of Christianity: at the Blessed Trinity.

V

It is true, of course, that this Biblical allowing of the
divine life to take possession of all one's actions is not
confined to the mystics alone but is for all Christians
—indeed, it is sometimes argued that the words of St.
Paul do not necessarily imply a mystical experience on
the part of the great apostle himself. But it so happens
that through the deeply experienced mystical life this
process of divinization is performed with greater thor-
oughness; it so happens that a strong love of God arising in the heart will often (even normally) express itself in a mystical way—that is, in "vertical thinking"
(for love tends to this downward plunge to the depths
of one's being); so the divinization becomes something
deeply felt, deeply experienced while being known by
faith—though it is certain that this divinization can be
effected also by a grace which comes not through mysticism but through suffering, abnegation, trials, and the
fidelity of an ordinary Christian life.

As for the kind of prayer that reflects on Christ as
He appears in the scriptures, Huxley is right in saying
that this was over-stressed at a certain period in Catholic history. It is true that the *Exercises* of Ignatius which
he specially impugns contain much of this; but they
were originally written for beginners coming in from the
world to a life of prayer, and they contain many sug-

gestions for initiating people to the life of prayer: that it was not the intention of their author that such people should spend their whole life in an analytical kind of prayer is abundantly clear from his other writings. Moreover, the fact that he makes ample use of the *Anima Christi*, with its humanistic mysticism of being inebriated with the blood of Christ and hiding within His wounds, shows that he was leading to something that analytical discourse will never fathom. And, again, there is some evidence to show that he was leading to a silent Pauline prayer at the climax of the *Exercises* from the fact that, at the climax, Christ (who all through has been central to the discursive meditations) almost disappears: the "Contemplation for Obtaining Divine Love" has little of Christ but only of God who is present in all creation, working for us. It seems to me that the absence of Christ can be explained only by the fact that Christ is no longer outside but within; and the exercitant, looking through the eyes of Christ at a world filled with God, makes an offering or a "Suscipe"—wherein Christ in the Christian offers Himself again to the Father for the redemption of the human race. Thus the *Exercises* end in silence: in a silent Trinitarian offering that is not so far removed from John of the Cross.

And that, in the last analysis, the humanity of Christ is not the supreme object of meditation is no more than the teaching of Aquinas who maintains that this humanity is the chief incentive to devotion "although devotion itself has for its principal object things that concern the Godhead."

VI

It goes without saying that the contemplative prayer of identification with Christ is incomparably higher and more valuable than the so-called discursive meditation. This latter, though it delighted the medievals (who liked to place themselves with Christ by the lake with

His disciples, listening to His words, resolving to imitate His virtues, and so on), seems to many modern people a little sophisticated and even fictitious—for we have no picture of Christ to tell us what He looked like and no guarantee that He actually spoke many of the words attributed to Him in the Gospels. Any serious Christian writer or director would agree that analytical thinking is only for beginners.

At the same time, Huxley's good-humoured attack on the Jesuits for hammering home analytical prayer to the exclusion of everything else is not without foundation. In the period after the death of Ignatius, those who governed the Society of Jesus (and especially the not-too-spiritually-competent General Roothaan) wrote dry-as-dust mathematical treatises about the three powers of the soul (memory, understanding, and will), evincing a wary distrust of anything that might savor of quietism or illuminism or any of the isms that were floating around at the time. While a great number of the rank and file seem to have possessed remarkable contemplative gifts, they seldom wrote about them; those who did (like Louis Lallemant) were duly squelched, thus paying the price for their indiscretion. The official stand of the Jesuits influenced the whole Church—hence one can understand Huxley's lament (however exaggerated) that Catholicism of the last century turned prayer into geometry.

One more point: Catholic writers have tended to stress a species of historical prayer tied to the Lake of Galilee and the synagogue at Capharnaum in reaction against a liberal theology that proclaimed our complete ignorance of the historical Christ. Directors felt obliged to be wary of the spirituality that said: "What matter about the Jesus who was born in Bethlehem! What matter if he never even existed! The important thing is the Jesus I meet in prayer." Such an idea is obviously destructive of Christianity (if it were true, one might just as well become the Buddha as become one with Jesus), and one can sympathize with the spiritual writers who repudiated it with such vigor. But some of them may well have emphasized Christ's historicity to the extent of toning down the Christ of faith who is now living, the resurrected Christ within the Christian, the Christ of whom Paul says, "I live, now not I, but Christ liveth in me." And it is this latter Christ (who is, of course, the same as the historical Christ) who occupies the central place in contemplative prayer.

Consequently, I would simply reiterate the point of this section; namely, that Aldous Huxley is right in saying that mysticism has nothing to do with analytical prayer and with meditation on persons and their qualities. Christian mysticism transcends all this. However, it is filled with Christ—present, not as object of meditation but within. One loses one's own consciousness to put on the consciousness of Christ. "Let that mind be in you which was in Christ Jesus. . . ." The Christian mysticism of John of the Cross effects a forgetting of self for union with Christ who is offering Himself to the Father in the Holy Spirit for the redemption of the world.

VII

No modern treatment of incarnation would be complete without a word about Teilhard de Chardin, mystic, scientist, and apostle of matter. The doubts that have been cast upon Teilhard's scientific speculations may be well-founded (about this I am not competent to judge); but if the mystic is one who has a supraconceptual sense of presence, a grasp of the unity of all things, a feeling for the penetration of the universe by God, then Teilhard's deeply mystical character cannot be questioned. He was a visionary in the literal sense of the word. He prefaces *The Phenomenon of Man* with an encomium of "seeing": ". . . the history of the living world can be summarised as the elaboration of ever more perfect eyes within a cosmos in which there is always something more to be seen." [4] To live is to see.

When one sees far enough into the material universe
one sees unity; even further one sees God; further still,
one sees Christ—for He, the cosmic Christ, is coexten-
sive with the universe. Scientist though he was, Teilhard wanted to see beyond the physical world; he
wanted to see with mystical eyes: ". . . the more I
look into myself the more I find myself possessed by the
conviction that it is only the science of Christ running
through all things, that is to say true mystical science,
that really matters." [5] "The veneer of color and place
bore me to tears. What I love cannot be seen." [6] What
Teilhard sees cannot be seen, for the light is darkness.
How near to Dionysius after all!

He seems to have had this mystical sense of cosmic
presence from an early age, though he himself could
not put his finger on the exact moment when it all
began. In *Le Milieu Divin* he refers to this consciousness of the omnipresent divine in words that could
have been written by a thousand mystics:

> On some given day a man suddenly becomes con-
> scious that he is alive to a particular perception of
> the divine spread everywhere about him. Question
> him. When did this state begin for him? He cannot
> tell. All he knows is that a new spirit has crossed his
> life.[7]

This sense of unity, so ineffable, introduces him to a
new dimension. "I had in fact acquired a new sense,
the sense of a new quality or *of a new dimension*.
Deeper still: a transformation had taken place for me
in the very perception of being." [8] I have italicized the
above words because they recall Jung's description of
entry into a new dimension. And this is what mysticism
is.

Teilhard's life was a struggle to reconcile this mystical experience with the dogmatic formulae of the faith
taught to him. Put in other words, the struggle of his
life was for the formulation of a mystical theology that
would satisfy him as a mystic, a scientist, and a human-

ist. He speaks of these "two axes—. . . only after much time and effort did I at last grasp . . . their connection, their convergence and finally their ultimate identity." [9] The conclusion he reached was that his cosmic sense was nothing else than the sense of Christ. "Quite specifically it is Christ whom we make or whom we undergo in all things." [10]

Like most mystics, he was misunderstood and criticized by the smaller men in the cave who, preoccupied with shadows, had no eyes for the glorious vision that he saw. But he clung to his vocation with heroic obstinacy; and at the end of his life we find him writing to his superior of a complete inability to deny his inner vision. "Everything stems from that basic psychological condition, and I can no more change it than I can change my age or the color of my eyes." [11] Indeed, he is a mystic for our time.

VIII

To understand Teilhard one must remember that as a Jesuit (and a good one at that) he belonged to a Society founded by a man who wanted to put together the seemingly contradictory occupations of contemplation and action. To a certain extent Ignatius succeeded; but many problems remained, only to become evident in our day—and chief among these was that of the whole meaning or value of human activity. For Ignatius all human work (whether sweeping the floor or looking through a microscope) had value if the intention of the subject was directed to God: for Teilhard the very activity had intrinsic value because it was a building of something—it was a building of the universe, a building of Christ, since evolution has put into human hands the work of cosmogenesis and even of Christogenesis. His mysticism leads straight out of the desert into the factory, the workshop, the classroom, the laboratory. In its deeply incarnational nature it diametrically opposes anything like Neoplatonic flight—and all this would surely have delighted the heart of Ignatius who was looking precisely for a reconciliation between the life of prayer and life in the world. Yet Teilhard loved solitude, too; and one of his most poetically magnificent works gives us a glimpse of this great mystic alone on the mountain (how like his Master), offering up the magnificent hymn of the Mass upon the altar of the universe. Or again, elsewhere, he dramatically appeals to Benson's description of the entire universe revolving around the silent figure of a tiny nun wrapped in contemplative prayer. In his very solitude Teilhard was united with matter, and through matter with Christ.

Ignatius' "Contemplation for Obtaining Divine Love" was a key influence in his life. It painted the kind of world vision that appealed to the young Chardin even before he entered the Society of Jesus: a world vibrating with the presence of God—and not only with His presence but also with His work and His action. Man of genius that he was, Teilhard shaped the Ignatian vision to his own Teilhardian mold, and the whole thing became alive with evolution, with growth, with building. Now, there is not only presence but also movement, not only being but also becoming. "To be in communion with becoming has become the formula of my whole life." [12] Everything is becoming and we are building, as the evolving universe moves on to greet Christ Omega at the *parousia.*

Teilhard's doctrine of the cosmic Christ has been the subject of considerable discussion. Some have interpreted it as meaning that all material things (the mountains and streams, the hills and the factories) are quite literally the body of Christ. But surely Teilhard could not have meant anything so absurd. He himself appeals to Paul in Ephesians and Colossians where Christ is the center of everything. "You are part of a building that has the apostles and prophets for its foundations, and Christ Jesus Himself for its main cornerstone." Or his thought can be summed up in the Johannine "But I, if I be lifted up from the earth, will draw all things to myself." The risen Jesus, lifted up in glory, draws the whole universe to Himself. He is the center; and because He is the center He fills the whole sphere.

If Teilhard had meant that every single thing is literally Christ's body he would have had no interest in the Eucharist (for the bread of life would be no different from any other bread), whereas we know that devotion to the Eucharist was one of the overmastering inspirations of his life. It is precisely through the Eucharist that the world is divinized.

> When Christ, extending the process of His incarnation, descends into the bread in order to replace it, His action is not limited to the material morsel which His presence will, for a brief moment, volatilize: this transubstantiation is aureoled with a real though attenuated divinizing of the entire universe. From the particular cosmic element into which He has entered, the activity of the Word goes forth to subdue and to draw into Himself all the rest.[13]

His argument about the divinization of the universe goes in two steps. First: the whole universe is for man, is gathered up in man, is spiritualized by man's knowledge to such an extent that "in each of us, through matter, the whole history of the world is in part reflected." [14] Further, there is, and can be, nothing without man; the notion that man can step back and look objectively at the universe is erroneous; he is in it and of it: he is involved.

Now, if the universe lives in man, the second step is not difficult for those who believe the scriptures. All men, united in Christ, are destined to make up the body of Christ. Teilhard spurns those who would whittle down the Pauline doctrine of the mystical body. "As a consequence of the Incarnation, the divine immensity has transformed itself for us into the omnipresence of Christification." [15] Jesus "suranimates" the world. "You have so filled the universe in every direction, Jesus, that henceforth it is blessedly impossible for us to escape you." [16] And from this springs the mystical marriage which climaxes *Le Milieu Divin*:

> Now the earth can certainly clasp me in her giant arms. She can swell me with her life, or draw me back into her dust. She can deck herself with every charm, with every horror, with every mystery. She can intoxicate me with her perfume of tangibility and unity. She can cast me to my knees in expectation of what is maturing in her breast.
>
> But her enchantments can no longer do me harm, since she has become for me, over and above herself, the body of Him who is and of Him who is coming. [17]

In this way, through the Eucharist, the universe is progressively divinized and Christified until the renewal of all things at the *parousia*.

Some have claimed that Teilhard's Christology is as old as St. Paul; others that it is as new as McLuhan. Certainly it is an interesting interpretation of Paul; and it does contain something that is new to Christian mystical theology—for (as I have pointed out) until Teilhard the body of Christ was not taken as the object of mystical contemplation; Christ was within and, taking over the body of the mystic, He looked through his eyes and blessed through his hands in such wise that the mystic's very flesh became "another Christ" loving the Father. Teilhard does at times come to this way of thinking, as, for example, when he writes that "in heaven we ourselves shall contemplate God but, as it were, through the eyes of Christ"; [18] or, again, in that hymn which is the mass of the universe, Christ's relationship with the Father is greatly in evidence. But, all in all, it can be said that Trinitarian theology (or the lack of it) is the Achilles' heel of the great man.

IX

Yet incarnational he was, through and through. His vision is always one of God seen through matter; of God made man, risen from the dead, living and growing in the material universe. Hence the value of everything that strikes the senses—of science, of progress, of all that is human.

But he was not (as has been suggested) the incurable optimist who forgot about suffering and sin. One who suffered as he did could not fail to grasp the value of purification, of detachment, of the cross; could not but see that there is no mysticism without a great death. What he needed was a new terminology in which to express it all; for the dark nights with the "nothing, nothing, nothing" of Mount Carmel could never appeal to one whose whole expression was filled with luxuriant richness, with a world on fire, ablaze, incandescent, vibrating, full of light. The apophatic darkness of the cloud is replaced by a radiant mysticism of "diaphany." Yet the Teilhardian light and the Dionysian darkness are less contradictory than might at first appear.

In both cases the aim (put positively) is love: put negatively, it is death to self; both point out the path to the divinization of man. In John of the Cross the whole thing is in a scholastic framework: the path of purification must be partly active (*The Ascent*), and partly passive (*The Dark Night*), and it transforms man according to the so-called "three powers of the soul" so that faith fills the intellect, hope the memory, and love the will. Death to self means life to Christ. In Teilhard, also, the purification is partly active (the divinization of our activities), partly passive (the divinization of our passivities), leading to an anguishing loss of self; but whereas John of the Cross' individualistic education makes him concentrate on the personal divinization of the mystic, Teilhard is preoccupied with the divinization of mankind and his universe. In John of the Cross I become Christ ("I live, now not I . . ."): in Teilhard the universe becomes Christ. And both demand the most frightful detachment. Teilhard uses this word less than does the great Spaniard, but its spirit permeates *Le Milieu Divin,* warning us that only through suffering can we grow in the purity and faith and love that builds up the universe into Christ.

Death, fearful and terrible, stands out in his work, becoming more and more starkly oppressive as the years advance. "In any event, all of us are growing old and all of us will die . . . ; we feel the constraining grip of the forces of diminishment, against which we were fighting, gradually gaining mastery over the forces of life, and dragging us physically vanquished to the ground. . . ."[19] Yet, the optimism of faith triumphs; and in words that strike that mystical chord common to all the great religions he tells us that the loss of self brings "the irresistible rise, in the depth of my consciousness, of some sort of Other, more me than myself."[20] (Here surely is language that the East understands.) And "the function of death is to provide the necessary entrance into our inmost selves"[21]—by it we "lose all foothold within ourselves" so that every ounce of selfishness is cleansed away. As I have said, the whole thing is ultimately not so far from John of the Cross. A rough formula covering the spirituality of both might run as follows: active and passive purification leading to love and divinization.

X

The unfortunate thing, however, is that Teilhard knew so little about John of the Cross and Aquinas. He practically ignores them—even though his childhood piety, containing all that is basic to Catholicism, remained with him to the end. One wonders how he spent his six or seven years of priestly studies when so little scholasticism went into his make-up. This is not to say that he should have been a dyed-in-the-wool scholastic (we all thank God that he was not); but it is easier to sympathize with a mystic who, having understood the traditional thought, rejects certain elements in it, or expresses it in different language according to the exigencies of scientific evolution, than with one who blissfully ignores the whole thing. Teilhard seems to have done something like this with the result that he considered his own experience quite unique. At the end of his life we find him writing:

> How is it, then, that I find myself in a class alone, as it were? Alone in having *seen*? . . . unable, when asked to do so, to instance a single author, a single writing, where there is a clearly expressed awareness of the amazing "diaphany" which, as I see it, transfigures everything? . . . The Christ of the universe? Le Milieu Divin? . . . May I not be, after all, at the mercy of a mirage within me? I often wonder.[22]

This is a surprising confession. For the fact is that plenty of mystics saw Teilhard's "amazing diaphany," though their interpretation and expression is somewhat different (less evolutionary and less Christological). He was not so alone as he imagined. If only he had been permitted to publish his thought, the response from kindred souls would no doubt have reassured him.

Furthermore, his attention would have been drawn to certain theological exaggerations in his mystical thinking. Chief among these is his tendency to make the body of Christ an absolute rather than (as in Aquinas) a means of devotion to the Godhead. Teilhard's whole system would have benefited from a Trinitarian framework; it would have held together more scripturally if Omega had been, not Christ, but the Father. Then we would have had a Johannine vision of Christ (who came out from God) returning to His Father in union with the human race and the evolving universe that we are building: Christ, leader of mankind and prime promoter of evolution, bringing us all to the Father in the Holy Spirit. And from this would spring the picture of a dynamic Church, the body of Christ, ever in a state of incompletion until the second coming, but increasingly divinized by the Eucharist while its members devote their lives to consecrating the world to the Father with Christ, His Son. With such a vision he would not have been alone. But even as it is, the Christ of the universe (albeit in modified form) will for ever occupy a place in Christian mystical theology.

NOTES

1. Aldous Huxley, *Grey Eminence* (New York, 1941), p. 101.
2. I am concerned here with the interpretation of Paul made by the mystics. Exegetes have different views on the matter.
3. Jung, *Psychology and Religion*, p. 546.
4. Pierre Teilhard de Chardin, s.j., *The Phenomenon of Man* (New York, 1961), "Foreword," p. 31.
5. Pierre Teilhard de Chardin, s.j., *Letters from a Traveller* (London, 1962), pp. 85–86.
6. *Ibid.*
7. Pierre Teilhard de Chardin, s.j., *Le Milieu Divin* (London, 1964), p. 128.
8. *Ibid.*, p. 129.
9. Christopher F. Mooney, s.j., *Teilhard de Chardin and the Mystery of Christ* (New York, 1966), p. 22.
10. Teilhard, *Le Milieu Divin*, p. 123.
11. Pierre Leroy, s.j., "Teilhard de Chardin: The Man," *ibid.*, p. 38. (This essay is also to be found in *Letters from a Traveller*, pp. 15–47.)
12. Teilhard, *Letters from a Traveller*.
13. Pierre Teilhard de Chardin, s.j., *Hymn of the Universe* (London, 1962), p. 14.
14. Teilhard, *Le Milieu Divin*, p. 59.
15. *Ibid.*, p. 123.
16. *Ibid.*, p. 127.
17. *Ibid.*, p. 155.
18. *Ibid.*, p. 143.
19. *Ibid.*, p. 85.
20. Pierre Teilhard de Chardin, s.j., *Le Christique* (unpublished; see Hubert Hoskins, "Teilhard de Chardin," *The Times* [London], October 14, 1967).
21. Teilhard, *Le Milieu Divin*, p. 89.
22. Teilhard, *Le Christique*.

10

ZEN AND THE WEST

I

In recent times much has been said and written about the cultural crisis in the West; not infrequently it has been suggested that beneath the surface of Western man there lurks some psychological disease that may well end up by destroying him. One of the first to point a finger at the imbalance of Western man was C. G. Jung, who loved to talk about the impoverishment of a West that has "lost its myth"; and more recently Karl Stern, following in the footsteps of the great psychologist, has revived the picture of a defeminized, dehumanized West, rich in technology but desperately poor in intuition, poor in the wisdom called *sophia*, and in what Dr. Stern himself calls "womanly values." Thus arises again the specter of a Nineteen Eighty-Four, of a brave new world of robots, of a waste land that is ever more sterile, of a West that is sick from lack of mysticism.

Granted that much of this talk contains exaggeration and even melodrama, it still remains true that the West has for some time been uneasily conscious of its own spiritual poverty. And it is just at this juncture that Zen Buddhism (particularly that of Dr. Suzuki) has made its appearance. Into the West has come a religion which is essentially mystical, placing all its emphasis on the enlightenment called *satori* and offering precisely those values which the West seems to lack. Small wonder that the appeal of "the mystic East" has made itself felt, and that not a few Westerners have turned their eyes to

Zen in search of something profound that may be able
to satisfy their deeper aspirations. Of the Westerners
who in recent years have turned to Zen, some have
been Christians dissatisfied with a Christianity that
often seems too rational, too Cartesian, and too juridi-
cal; often these people have never had any real *experience* of Christianity—which, in consequence, seems
hollow by comparison with the depth of Zen. It may be
that they have been ignorant of the mystical element in
Christianity; for it is well known that both Catholics
and Protestants have been suspicious of (even hostile
toward) mysticism. Catholics have voiced fears about
pantheism and quietism; Protestants sometimes look at
Western mysticism as a Neoplatonic invasion contam-
inating the pure and limpid stream that flows from the
Bible. So it is hardly surprising that people in search
of mysticism should be propelled toward the East.

II

Confronted with the phenomenon of Zen, various Western attitudes can be observed. The first is that of some
rather traditionalist theologians who have not hesitated
to classify it with convenient labels such as "monism"
or "pantheism," or to say that it is a form of "quietism."
It should be noted, however, that all these terms are
taken from Western thought and are never used by the
Zen people themselves. This kind of classification stems
from an attempt to draw Zen on to Western ground
and to speak of it in Western categories. Furthermore
it recalls the words used about mystics like Eckhart
and Madame Guyon, and we cannot forget that the
word "pantheism" was bandied about in regard to Teilhard de Chardin. Certainly it is a vague enough word,
even though it may seem at first sight to be admirably
suited to describe a Zen that speaks of one's identity
with the universe, or of the loss of self, or of the non-self
condition, and so on.

Yet some more recent Christian writers have come to

the prudent conclusion that it is better to take Zen on
its own ground and that any attempt to squeeze it into
Western categories is necessarily doomed to failure. "We
have read our Western divisions into an Oriental experience that has nothing whatever to do with them,"
writes Thomas Merton in a recent work, "and we have
also presumed that Oriental contemplation corresponds
in every way with Western philosophical modes of contemplation and spirituality. Hence the mystifying use of
terms like 'individualism,' 'subjectivism,' 'pantheism,' etc.
. . . Actually these terms are worse than useless. . . .
They serve to make Zen utterly inaccessible." [1] And
then, with remarkable insight, Merton goes on to state
that Zen is in fact "the ontological awareness of pure
being beyond subject and object, an immediate grasp of
being in its 'suchness' and 'thisness.'" [2]

Much misunderstanding of Zen Buddhism arises from
a Western failure to understand that almost all its language is primarily phenomenological or descriptive and
that when it speaks of "becoming the object" or "becoming the universe" this is no more than a description of
a psychological experience of identification which is
deeply embedded in all Japanese culture. (Though it is
not limited to Japan alone, and I have pointed to something similar in T. S. Eliot and in Jung.) What precisely
this experience of identity means in the ontological order
need not concern us here; suffice it to remark that not
all Zennists will deny the existence of a transcendent
God. Dr. D. T. Suzuki never tires of saying that Zen
neither affirms nor denies God—it is indifferent to God.
And Père Charles grasped this in advance of his times
when he remarked: "In neither of the two vehicles has
the place of God been usurped. It is empty, like a pedes-
tal without a statue." For it should be noted that Buddhism does not begin with a Genesis-like affirmation of
the existence of God or of anything else: rather, it is a
search or quest for a wisdom which comes only at the
end, as a climax—nor is it impossible that this quest
might end in a discovery of God. At all events, people

who have had some experience of speaking with Zen masters have found that while God has no place in the scheme of things His existence is not always excluded. Consequently, some Zen masters seem to have a sense of a transcendent Being (even though they may not call this being "God" or "Kami"), while others have not. Anyone who speaks to Zen monks soon finds that they speak constantly about the "sense of gratitude," so that the Westerner immediately asks "Gratitude to whom?" —to which question, however, there is usually no answer. One Buddhist simply remarked to me that Christians speak about God while Buddhists do not. Enomiya-Lasalle, too, insisting that much confusion arises from verbal misunderstanding and that it can be dispelled by dialogue, writes of an enlightened monk who firmly believed in God and declared: "Everything is denied, but in the distance one sees God." Such a statement would delight the heart of St. John of the Cross.

As for the charge of quietism, anyone who has even a little knowledge of Zen knows that it entails the most tremendous concentration imaginable. If "Quietism" means some kind of idling, then it has nothing to do with Zen. In fact, the literature of Zen is filled with attacks on idle waste of time during the silent meditation —attacks which are no less vehement than those found in Christianity.

From all this it can be seen how desirable it is to drop Western philosophical terminology and to take Zen on its own ground, using existential and descriptive words. If this is done, dialogue can be instituted; and indeed this very dialogue has begun in Japan with considerable prospects of mutual understanding and appreciation.

III

I have mentioned certain theologians who have manifested a distrust of Zen and its so-called "pantheistic" tendencies. One might ask, then, what is to be thought of the more enthusiastic people who want to take into the West the rigorous Zen meditation just as it is—with its long periods of squatting, its meager diet, its submission to the guidance of the master; for it is well known that Zen centers are springing up in Europe and America in which Zen is practiced according to the traditional Japanese pattern.

Now, it seems to me that while Japanese Zen may be of great value to certain individual Westerners (one could cite the examples of Ruth Sasaki or Philip Kapleau) its value for Western people at large is greatly open to question. This, at all events, was the opinion of Jung, who rated Zen very highly but deprecated its use in the West. "Great as is the value of Zen Buddhism for understanding the religious transformation process," he wrote, "its use among Western people is very problematic." [3] He held that the mental education necessary for Zen was lacking in the West and that a direct transplantation to Western conditions was neither commendable nor possible. This, in fact, was Jung's attitude toward much of Eastern thinking, and it is worth quoting a passage where he speaks of Yoga in words which express clearly enough what he thought also about Zen in the West:

> If I remain so critically averse to yoga, it does not mean that I do not regard this spiritual achievement of the East as one of the greatest things the human mind has ever created. I hope my exposition makes it sufficiently clear that my criticism is directed solely against the application of yoga to the peoples of the West. The spiritual development of the West has been along entirely different lines from that of the East and has therefore produced conditions which are the most unfavourable soil one can think of for the application of yoga. Western civilization is scarcely a thousand years old and must first of all free itself from its barbarous one-sidedness. This means, above all, deeper insight into the nature of man. But no insight is gained by repressing and controlling the unconscious, and least of all by imitating methods

which have grown up under totally different psychological conditions. In the course of the centuries the
West will produce its own yoga, and it will be on
the basis laid down by Christianity.[4]

Jung esteemed Yoga and Zen very highly (indeed he
sometimes spoke of them with an enthusiasm bordering
on the naïve) but he was adamantly opposed to their indiscriminate use in the West.

Nor is Jung alone. The Western interest in Zen has
intrigued (and even amused) quite a number of Japanese people; and quite recently an eminent Japanese
psychiatrist has examined this phenomenon, coming up
with interesting conclusions. I have already referred to
Dr. Takeo Doi who maintains that lonely Western man
has developed his ego too much, finds that he can no
longer cope with the situation he has created, feels an
ever-growing insecurity, and looks for a solution in the
non-ego condition of Zen. He seems to think that Zen is
healthy if one breaks through to *satori*. But many do
not. Instead, they break down mentally. Moreover,
many, he maintains, experience an illusory state of liberation from the dust of the world, a state which is an
escapist denial of reality akin to that induced by LSD
and marijuana. This is particularly evident in those who
go in for the cult of Zen—for the boom and the fad.
Dr. Doi is skeptical of what he calls "the cult of emptiness." And if all these dangers exist for the Japanese,
how much more so for the man from the West!

Zen meditation is the outcome of centuries of tradition. It is not surprising that these two psychologists
(one European and the other Japanese) would call into
question its direct transplantation to the cultural climate
of the West.

IV

In fact, however, the most obviously modern approach
to Zen is dialogue. Without making hasty judgments and

without abandoning their respective positions, both sides can talk and they can learn. And in this way something fruitful for both can emerge. At the same time, since to talk to Zen people is always problematic (often they prefer not to talk, or if they do so their speech is filled with paradox), a dialogue should be carried on at the level of mystical or artistic experience. For it is here that a common denominator can be found.

And here it is interesting to note that probably the most successful attempts at understanding dialogue have been made less by the Orientalists than by men of letters. One person, for example, who spoke a language that Japan understands is W. B. Yeats—who was no scholar in anything Oriental but who had an intuitive grasp of things Japanese that has earned him a wide reputation in this country.[5] Let me give one small example of his understanding of the Zen way of thinking. In his *Certain Noble Plays of Japan,* he remarks that "We only believe those thoughts which have been conceived not in the brain but in the whole body." [6] This is a significant insight. For it is well known that the Western approach to life (owing so much to the Greeks) is intellectual, cerebral, syllogistic. In the realm of prayer, for instance, spiritual writers have ingeniously analyzed man's memory, understanding, and will: but they have had little to say about his breathing, his abdomen, his eyes, and his hands. The East, on the other hand, still remembers that man can adore God with his whole body, and has developed methods of concentration that go back to prehistoric days. And from all this, the West can learn much. For surely, as Yeats so truly remarks, the notional assent given to the conclusion of a syllogism often has little real motive power in a man's life and may be lightly cast aside in moments of emotional crisis; but the conviction conceived in the whole body is less easily lost. If the faith of many a modern Catholic were rooted in the body, it might be less lightly abandoned in his moments of agonized isolation when, like a terrified child, lonely and crushed by the vast universe of outer space, he feels that everything he believed is slipping through his fingers.

Side by side with Yeats stands T. S. Eliot who, again, is a big name in Japanese literary circles. Like Yeats he, too, was no Orientalist; but he was interested. Professor Masao Hirai of Tokyo University tells the somewhat amusing story of how he went to visit Eliot at Faber and Faber with many questions about the major poems; but he got no opportunity to ask anything—because Eliot kept plying him with questions about Zen Buddhism.[7] It is not only the meeting of St. Augustine and the Buddha in the torrid waste land—but from his early days Eliot was interested in the intuitive moment, the moment that shakes the universe, the moment in which one touches the still point of the turning world. And all this is unmistakably similar to the enlightenment of Zen. This is not to say that Eliot was greatly influenced by Buddhism (the dominant influence in the mysticism of his later years is clearly St. John of the Cross), but he saw the parallel and initiated the dialogue—a dialogue which was so eminently successful that on his death a book was immediately written in his honor, adding to the large bibliography of Japanese books already dedicated to his work.[8] Furthermore, he seems to have felt deeply and personally the same problems as the East—problems of time and eternity, of human anxiety, of the cycle of the turning world. And is there not a trace of Buddhist (rather than Christian) detachment in the characters of Becket and Celia and Colby?

In short, Eliot, while remaining Western (and incorrigibly so), has seen parallels between the two worlds, has pointed the way to dialogue, has learned much from the East, has been stimulated by Buddhism to reinvestigate the riches of the Western mystical tradition.

V

All this naturally leads to the problem of the influence of Zen Buddhism on Western Christianity. Recent times have witnessed a certain amount of discussion about the possibility of a Catholic Zen or a Christian Yoga; and several studies have been made on this subject. These have been partly stimulated by the general post-conciliar humility of a Catholic Church eager to learn from all good religions and assuring her children that cordial investigation of the spiritual values of non-Christians is no longer the prerequisite of a few barely tolerated pioneers but a solemn duty imposed upon the Church at large. But they have also been influenced by the real crisis in prayer (part of the general cultural crisis to which I referred at the beginning) which makes people feel, like de Foucauld, that there may be a solution hidden in the mystical tradition of the East. It is not precisely that modern Christians do not want to pray (the popularity of the mystics from Merton to Dag Hammarskjöld would indicate that they do), but that they are too nervous to pray. "Teach us to sit still." The tempo of life with its crisis upon crisis has created the neurotic uneasiness so conspicuous in modern life. While meditative, discursive prayer is thus rendered difficult, it may well be that there is a certain yearning for a simplified approach to God. At all events, within the Catholic Church the Carmelite mystics are much in vogue; while Christianity at large joins Bishop Robinson and Teilhard de Chardin in the search for a God who is the core of one's being, the ground of the soul, the essence of all things—in short, the immanent God of the mystics, God who is at the very heart of matter. And if one wants direction in the type of concentration demanded by this simplified approach, it is to the East that one should turn; for, as I have indicated, in the question of technique in simplified, contemplative thought, the West is in its infancy.

I would suggest, then, that the Zen technique can teach the Christian how to relax, how to be calm, how to think in a deeper way, how to dispose himself to receive God's love, how to conceive the truths of faith not only in his brain but in his whole body. To what extent it could lead to the so-called infused contemplation I have discussed already, saying that the old distinction between "acquired" and "infused" or between prayer "which can be taught" and "that which cannot" is of doubtful validity. It is not impossible that Eastern techniques can teach more mysticism than nineteenth-century spiritual direction dreamed possible. This is a question which I shall treat tentatively in the next chapter.

NOTES

1. Thomas Merton, *Mystics and Zen Masters* (New York, 1967), pp. 16 ff.
2. *Ibid.*, p. 14.
3. Jung, *Psychology and Religion*, p. 537.
4. *Ibid.*
5. "This country," of course, refers to Japan, where this book was written. There is a Yeats Society in Japan claiming members from universities throughout the country. One of its prominent members is Shotaro Oshima, known for his *W. B. Yeats and Japan* (Tokyo, 1965).
6. W. B. Yeats, *Certain Noble Plays of Japan.*
7. Though Professor Hirai admires Eliot very much, it must be confessed that he is a little skeptical about the depths of his knowledge of Buddhism. He writes: "So far as 'The Fire Sermon' is concerned, it seemed to me that Eliot made use of the image of 'burning' just for the sake of the image, regardless of whether or not he could believe what the image stood for. He may have inserted these words just because he thought they could occupy an aesthetically adequate and proper place in a poetic context which corresponded exactly to his complicated mental condition at that time. One might as well find here one of those cases in which 'mature poets steal.' But how far and whether he, as a Christian, committed himself, even temporally, to the Buddhist doctrine seemed to be a matter of conjecture" ("T. S. Eliot and the Idea

of Wisdom" in Masao Hirai and E. W. F. Tomlin, eds., *T. S. Eliot: A Tribute from Japan* [Tokyo, 1966], p. 20).
8. The above-mentioned book contains a six-page bibliography of Japanese translations of Eliot's work, together with books and articles about him published in Japan.

11

ZEN AND CHRISTIANITY

I

In the last chapter I quoted Jung to the effect that Zen has its roots deep in an Oriental tradition wholly different from that of the West, and that, in consequence, slavish imitation of Zen by Westerners is somewhat problematic—even though, in individual cases, Europeans and Americans have found help and strength in its methods. I then advocated dialogue.

Now, such dialogue has begun tentatively in Japan. Here, however, the encounter is not so much between East and West as between a Buddhist East and a Christian East—since, obviously enough, Japanese Christians share the cultural heritage of their Buddhist compatriots. Moreover, dialogue is dialogue; it is not proselytizing, nor is it a theological attempt to prove that deep down all Buddhists are anonymous Christians. It is an attempt at mutual understanding, an encounter in charity, a search for common ground. And yet, interestingly enough, when one looks for this common ground the most insuperable barriers seem to arise, and one wonders if there is even one tenet on which both sides can agree. The existence of God, the immortality of the soul, the validity of logic—even on these most basic issues one will seldom get an unqualified consensus of the Buddhist and the Christian if the problem is stated in this Western way. Ultimately some formulae will be found on which there can be unanimity of opinion; but, in the meanwhile, is the gulf that separates us unbridgeable?

I should say not. From what has been said already it will be clear that there is one point of contact—namely, religious experience. The Christian with some depth in prayer and experience of the things of God will find himself in wonderful sympathy with the monk who has practiced Buddhist meditation. There is undoubtedly something in common between John of the Cross and the Buddha; and the Christian will find interior guidance in much Buddhist literature, just as John of the Cross points out the way to not a few Buddhists. This is because the psychic life of man is everywhere the same; his fundamental aspirations vary but little. Put more concretely, what is common to both is vertical thinking, the supraconceptual grasp of reality without words or concepts or images, the superthinking about which I have said so much. People who know what it means to meditate vertically in supraconceptual silence will understand one another. Dr. D. T. Suzuki and Thomas Merton found themselves in extraordinary harmony. Here, at the level of mysticism, East meets West. Here is the still point of the turning world.

II

In this chapter, however, it is not my intention to talk about dialogue, but rather to examine another problem —namely, the extent to which Zen can influence Christian prayer in Japan. We know that Christianity has made no small impact on Buddhism (think of Suzuki's grasp of Eckhart and the mystics), and this leads us to ask how far the reverse is also possible.

Which, in turn, raises the age-old problem of adaptation. Although we often say that everyone from the time of Xavier and Valignano has worked for an indigenous Church in Japan, it is clear that Japanese Christianity is still a foreign product, largely because it has been practically untouched by such religious and cultural trends as Zen—and this is in great measure responsible for its failure and for the mental torment that

has raged since the time of Meiji in the minds of so
many intellectuals who have hopelessly endeavored to
reconcile their national character with their Christianity. This mental conflict has already been graphically
described by the Catholic novelist, Endo Shusaku; here
it is sufficient to say that if Christianity is to be truly
Japanese and to satisfy the deepest aspirations of the
people in this country, it is difficult to see how it can
escape the influence of something that has extended
itself not only to the tea ceremony, flower arrangement,
archery, and all forms of Japanese culture, but to
every section of Japanese life.

But having said this, I would like to stress that
words like "Christian Zen" and "Zen Catholicism" must
be handled with care lest they lead to confusion. At
present, some Christians in Japan do sit in the lotus
posture going through a form of silent meditation that
shows the influence of Zen. This can be called Christian
Zen, but it should be remembered that the underlying
philosophy and the interior dispositions are totally different from those of Buddhism. Some masters are aware
of this and they dignify this Christian Zen with the
name of "gedo" or unorthodox Zen, but none would
say that it is what is practiced in the temple. For, in
the last analysis, Christians and Buddhists agree that
meditation is not totally divorced from one's philosophy
of life. Even though it is sometimes said "It doesn't
matter what you believe: just sit!" one must sit (I will
be forgiven for repeating it) on a philosophy of life.
One, of course, is detached from the words and concepts and images in which this philosophy is couched;
but it is there. The popular Western notion that Zen
throws all faith and philosophy out the window to sit
on literal emptiness arises partly from a misunderstanding of Suzuki's hyperbole. The Christian contemplative
and the Zen monk have each his own philosophy: they
sit on different *zabutons*.

Be that as it may, the question I want to ask here is:
To what extent can vertical meditation, so highly de-

veloped in the East, be introduced into Christian prayer? Is it possible to *teach* to Christians a prayer that is imageless, silent, and vertical, which will unify the personality in radical detachment from all things?

III

From what has been said earlier in this book it will be clear that while I am alive to the dangers of false mysticism and illusion, I am also convinced of the value of vertical meditation properly understood and that I favor its cultivation. Let me briefly recall some of its benefits.

First of all, I have said that this silent concentration lends depths to the personality, that it strengthens convictions, that it puts things into the whole body in a psychosomatic way, and that man is convinced of ideas that he conceives, not just in his brain, but in his whole body.

Again, I have tried to prove that vertical meditation leads to that serene detachment and interior liberty which is the hallmark of Buddhist art and Buddhist culture. Now, there was never an age in which inner freedom was so necessary as today when (as McLuhan reminds us) man is subjected to the tyranny of mass media and finds himself more and more hopelessly enmeshed in his own extended nervous system. Vertical meditation prevents one from getting all entangled. Not that it makes one blind and deaf; but it enables one to see and hear without enervating emotional involvement. Man can somehow step outside time, thus escaping from the hustling Heraclitean stream that sweeps him off his feet.

And, more than this, it liberates the mind from inordinate desires and distractions, enabling it to seek the deepest truth lying at the heart of reality. For the mind, of its very nature, stretches out toward truth, toward ultimate truth; but the turmoil of Babylon with the neon lights of our troubled century has obstructed this great quest. Take away the distractions; turn off the neon lights; reduce the turmoil—and the mind will find itself impelled toward the essence of things in order to find enlightenment. In other words, vertical meditation creates the detachment that allows the mind to go out to truth—and, Christians would say, to God.

Again, I have tried to show that vertical meditation promotes psychic growth and emotional maturity. Nor do we need Teilhard to remind us that man has a duty to grow, to mature, to pass from childhood through adolescence and on to manhood without getting stuck in infantilism. It is precisely vertical meditation that carries man forward at the time when categories and formulae get fossilized.

As for its relationship to prayer in the strict sense of this word, before considering this we must revise our conventional ideas of what prayer is. I have already referred to the nineteenth-century tendency to look on Christian prayer as a means to the acquisition of virtue: spiritual writers (and especially Jesuits) kept stressing that "meditation" should culminate in a practical resolution to be good or kind or humble or whatever it may be. Or prayer was looked upon as a means to an external imitation of Christ, a means to leading a life like His. Now, while no one should deny the value of such meditation for beginners, Huxley was right in his claim that it was overstressed to the exclusion of what was truly and deeply mystical. This kind of prayer, in fact, fails to satisfy many people after the age of thirty-five or forty (Jung's middle period), and unless their prayer starts to simplify they begin to ask why they should pray at all. They begin to question the relevance of it all; for "irrelevance" is the bogey of the modern religious man.

Now, the vertical type of meditation labors less under these difficulties, so that one is tempted to ask if it might not contain the answer to many of our problems. For one thing, it frequently appeals to people precisely in the tumultuous middle period when dis-

cursive prayer is losing its appeal; it holds promise of
tiding man over this most critical time of life. Furthermore, it has a clear-cut goal (what Ignatius called the
"id quod volo") which is enlightenment stemming from
a radical detachment from all things. People can go to
prayer in the belief that they will get something out of
it, that it will deepen their lives, that they will find
strength. In fine, it shows promise of being relevant.

IV

All this indicates that vertical meditation is a beneficial
discipline of the mind, a spiritual training of surpassing
human value—something that the East has discovered,
developed, and systematized, whereas the West has
stumbled upon it in certain cases, almost by accident.
As a method of concentration it can scarcely be neg-
lected, especially by those who are temperamentally
disposed to be permeated by its deepening silence. But
we have not yet shown its relevance for a specifically
Christian prayer centered on Christ and His Father.
One might say, of course, that it is a good *preparation*
in that it calms the mind, rendering it open to an awareness of God. But can it be more?

First of all, I should say that the Oriental technique
can deepen the prayer life of those who are already
contemplative. Much of the Zen technique will help
them practice the counsel of the mystics to abandon
thoughts and images in order that the tiny flame of
contemplative love may arise in the heart. "Forsake as
well good thoughts as evil thoughts," writes the author
of *The Cloud*. "And look that nothing remains in thy
working mind but a naked intent stretching unto God,
not clothed in any special thought of God in himself,
how he is in himself, or in any of his works, but only
that he is as he is." To allow this "naked intent" (John
of the Cross's "living flame of love") to take possession
of the heart there is probably no better physical pos-

ture than the cross-legged sitting and the upright position—in which discursive thinking is automatically
checked, and the mind is brought into that void where
contemplative love (if it incipiently exists) will rise up
and flourish. I believe that John of the Cross and those
like him would have welcomed the Zen technique with
joy—though they would only have prescribed it for
those in whose prayer the living flame of love has
begun to play a part. And much more would they have
welcomed the whole process of radical detachment—
though, again, they would have looked on this as no
more than a removal of what might impede divine
charity.

It could be safely argued, then, that anyone who has
spent a number of years in ordinary prayer might
profitably attempt some kind of vertical meditation in
the expectation that a latent contemplation, buried
deep in the heart, might spontaneously arise. Too many
potential contemplatives smother the tiny flame of love
with endless thinking, when they should be silent,
empty, and expectant.

But what about *satori*? Might the Christian contemplative come to an enlightenment similar to that of the
Buddhist?

In his book, Enomiya-Lasalle writes of a monk who
told him that the practice of Zen would lead to a
Christian enlightenment. And obviously it is this (if it
exists) that the Christian should aim at. Yet Christmas
Humphreys in a review of Lasalle's book expresses
doubts about such a possibility. While generously prais-
ing the pioneering spirit of the author, Mr. Humphreys
asserts that *satori* cannot come to the Christian because
he necessarily clings to ideas, dogmas, and beliefs. "He
[Father Enomiya-Lasalle] could not in the circumstances of his calling leave behind him dogmas and doc-
trinal premises. He could not empty his mind of
thoughts when rooted in it were his 'views,' as the
Buddhist would call them, on God." [1] In short, Chris-

tianity demands fidelity to ideas of God, of the Bible, of dogma—all which are an obstacle to enlightenment in utter nakedness.

I, however, should beg to differ here with Mr. Humphreys—whose view is basically the same as that of Aldous Huxley already mentioned. "In the circumstances of his calling" the Christian is not at all obliged to cling to views and ideas of God or of anything else. He must cling to God of course (for God is his truest being); but he need not (and, if he is a mystic, he ought not) cling to views and ideas about God. Contemplative prayer demands the rejection of concepts of God; and John of the Cross asks for the most rigorous detachment from all thoughts, ideas, and images of any kind, as well as from all formulations of dogma. This is not to say that these ideas and views are erroneous (I have made this point already and need not belabor it), but simply that they are imperfect and should be transcended when superthinking enters the conscious mind. Eckhart can speak of being so poor that one does not even "have a God."

All this, however, does not figure too much in popular Christianity—a fact which may have led Mr. Humphreys and Aldous Huxley to their conclusion—but in the mystics it is as plain as a pikestaff. However, it must be conceded that in Christian spiritual direction as it has existed until now, voiding the mind has been for mystics and for mystics only—not for the rank and file. Hence it has come later than in Zen; cessation of thinking has been permitted only when the mind is so saturated with Biblical and dogmatic truth that ordinary thought is no longer possible. For this reason also, detachment from thinking is probably more difficult for the Christian (the author of *The Cloud* keeps harping on the agony of the man who has abandoned concepts and reasoning): ideas and views have entered his psychic life so deeply that it is hard indeed to "let go." But to say that the Christian cannot transcend verbal expression of dogma would contradict not only the facts but the very dogmas themselves.

It seems to me, then, that the kind of *satori* resulting from an utter detachment from all things making one fall into the void is not impossible for the Christian. I do not say that his is the same as that of the Buddhist, but merely that it is induced by a somewhat similar psychological process. If it comes, it should be received with gratitude.

V

Yet, obviously, to find the true Christian *satori* one must turn to the Gospels where, indeed, we find constant talk of enlightenment and of the blind who see because of Jesus who is the light of the world. "The eye is the lamp of the body. So, if your eye is sound, your whole body will be full of light; but if your eye is not sound, your whole body will be full of darkness. If then the light in you is darkness, how great is the darkness!"

The Gospel developed in a Greco-Roman world and a Europe that often subordinated the great Christian awakening to legalism and ethics; but had the Gospel moved East instead of West, surely enlightenment would quickly have found an interpretation akin to that of Buddhism. The pearl of great price and the treasure hidden in the field might have been Christian enlightenment, and the Christian life could have been oriented to *seeing*.

No Buddhist denies that Christ was a deeply enlightened man. He saw things so differently from His contemporaries that they killed Him. He was the Zen master when He curtly told a would-be disciple to let the dead bury their dead, or when He told them to render to Caesar the things that are Caesar's, or when He enigmatically wrote on the ground so that they all went out, beginning with the eldest. And, as Jesus is the light of the world, so the follower must come to see things as His master does.

And from those who would come to this awakening He asked the most rigorous detachment: He wanted a great death. "Unless the grain of wheat falling into the ground dies, itself alone remains; but if it dies, it brings forth much fruit." To be the disciple of Jesus one must die; one must sell what one has and give to the poor; one must renounce "everything that he possesses" (and here John of the Cross insists that "everything" means just *everything*); one must hate father and mother and his own life also.

This is not to say that the enlightenment is necessarily a soul-stirring shock accompanied by a sudden transformation (though it may at times be just that); but it *is* a deep experience and a true change of consciousness. It reaches its climax when one's ego is lost to be replaced by that of Christ: "I live, now not I, but Christ liveth in me"; when one's consciousness is lost to be replaced by that of Christ: "Let that mind be in you which was in Christ Jesus"; it reaches its climax in a Trinitarian experience. "Now this is eternal life that they may know Thee the One true God and Jesus Christ whom Thou has sent."

About this I have written in earlier chapters where I spoke of the path along which the Christian mystic walks. To what extent a somewhat similar path could be found by a vertical meditation like Zen is something which no one yet knows. It has to be tried out; exploration has to be done; the pioneers have to do their difficult work. For this is an empirical field, and we have yet to discover how much of the so-called infused contemplation can be taught, how far technique can take us along the road, how an Oriental Christian prayer will differ from the traditional mysticism of the apophatic school. The experiment is being tried: history will give the answer.

One thing, however, is certain: mysticism is a vitally important phenomenon without which no religion can flourish. In her dealings with the East, Western Christianity must humbly admit that she has much to learn. If she does this, she will find her encounter with the Orient no less enriching than her meeting with Greco-Roman thought in the early years of her existence.

NOTE

1. Christmas Humphreys, "A Jesuit Looks at Zen," *The Catholic Herald,* June 2, 1967.

INDEX